William Henry Comyns

Exercises on a Series of Abstracts of Title to Freehold

Copyhold, and Leasehold Estates, and Personalty

William Henry Comyns

Exercises on a Series of Abstracts of Title to Freehold
Copyhold, and Leasehold Estates, and Personalty

ISBN/EAN: 9783337225100

Printed in Europe, USA, Canada, Australia, Japan

Cover: Foto ©ninafisch / pixelio.de

More available books at **www.hansebooks.com**

EXERCISES

ON A SERIES OF

ABSTRACTS OF TITLE

TO

FREEHOLD, COPYHOLD,

AND LEASEHOLD ESTATES,

AND PERSONALTY,

WITH

OBSERVATIONS AND REQUISITIONS ON
EACH TITLE.

ARRANGED AS EXERCISES FOR THE USE OF LAW STUDENTS
AND ARTICLED CLERKS, BY W. H. COMYNS.

London:
HAUGHTON & Co., 10, PATERNOSTER ROW.

1873.

LONDON:
PRINTED BY JAS. TRUSCOTT AND SON,
Suffolk Lane, City.

PREFACE.

In the acquisition of a knowledge of any art or science, and of the principles and rules having reference, and being applicable, to it, and a competent knowledge of which principles and rules is essential to be acquired by the student, a combination of practice with theory will (when attainable) much contribute to impress on the memory the purport and effect of such principles and rules, and of the conclusions and deductions which have been drawn and will be requisite to be deduced from them.

To the experienced practitioner it will be evident that a series of progressive practical abstracts of ordinary every-day titles, with explanatory observations and notes applicable to the peculiar subject of each title, would much aid the student in attaining a knowledge of the present complicated system of Law prevailing in this country relating to titles to real and personal property, and of the evidence and proofs requisite to be called for, or guarded against, in the examination and deduction of titles.

Most of the abstracts comprised in the following pages have been prepared and arranged as easy problems and exercises for the instruction of students, and considerable information and benefit have been derived from them by a numerous class. Endeavour has been made to render the abstracts useful by explanatory observations, notes, requisitions, and opinions.

When the student has read carefully the second

volume of the Commentaries of Sir William Blackstone, with modern notes, and the recent excellent works by Mr. William Hayes, and Mr. Joshua Williams, and other eminent members of the Bar, he will, in most cases, be in a position to comprehend with facility the greater part of the titles deduced in the abstracts and the observations thereon.

During the last forty years many important alterations and improvements have been effected in the system of Law relating to real and personal property by various statutory enactments; but as titles are in most cases (except under special stipulations) required to be deduced for sixty years at least, it yet remains necessary for the practitioners to be conversant with the Law as it prevailed before the passing of the modern statutes.

In each title the student will assume that the abstract is to be perused and considered on the part of a purchaser, or mortgagee, or of a vendor; and that the proper requisitions, conditions, or stipulations (as the case may be) are to be prepared for carrying the object contemplated into effect, and to relieve the purchaser or vendor (as the case may be) from unreasonable costs in the production and furnishing of documentary and other evidences and proofs of title which may not be absolutely necessary, and which in many instances may be safely waived or dispensed with. But it must be kept in mind that the waiving the production of evidence in support of an abstract of title must in each case depend on the peculiar circumstances of the title, the magnitude of the transaction, and the necessity or wish of the purchaser to complete the purchase.

Mr. Butler observes: "There can be no doubt but that the precautions taken for the security of a purchaser appear to be excessive, and satisfactory reasons cannot always be given for requiring some of them; yet the more experience any professional person acquires the more he feels the reason and real utility of them, and the more he will be convinced that very few of the precautions required by the general practice of the profession are without their use, or can be safely dispensed with."

For the sake of brevity, and to avoid a repetition of dates and references, the important modern Acts will in this work in most cases be referred to by the following letters, viz. :—

3 & 4 W. 4, cap. 27 (Limitation of Actions) . Act A.
3 & 4 W. 4, cap. 74 (Abolition of Fines and Recoveries) . . . . Act B.
3 & 4 W. 4, cap. 105 (Dower) . . . . . Act C.
3 & 4 W. 4, cap. 106 (Law of Inheritance) . Act D.
7 W. 4, and 1 Vic., cap. 26 (Wills) . . . Act E.
4 & 5 Vic. cap. 21 (Lease and Release) . . Act F.
8 & 9 Vic., cap. 106 (Conveyancing) . . . . Act G.
8 & 9 Vic., cap. 112 (Outstanding and Satisfied Terms) . . . . Act H.
22 & 23 Vic., cap. 35 (Act to Amend Law of Property) . . . . Act I.
23 & 24 Vic., cap. 38 (Act to further Amend Law of Property) . . . . Act K.

INDEX.

	PAGE
Acknowledgment of deed by married woman—Office copy of certificate to be furnished to purchaser	143
Administration suit—Policy 79,	157
Alien—Certificate of naturalization	167
Annuitant—Succession duty on death of 115, 141, 159,	160
Probate of will, or letters of administration, to be produced	115
Bank of England—Application to be made to Chief Accountant	142
Form of letter	144
Bankrupt—Office copies of proceedings to be furnished to purchaser	158
Base fee—Where protector does not concur in disentail..............37,	133
Benefit building society—Copy of rules to be furnished	168
As to stamp on mortgage	168
Clauses in Acts as to mortgages	170
Endorsement on mortgages 111, 168,	170
Chancery proceedings—As to production and office copies	126
Matters of record	127
Conditional mortgage surrender out of court and out of manor	12
Satisfaction to be entered on court roll	137
Copyhold—Equitable estate tail barred by deed	103
Deed to be entered on court rolls within six months from date and execution	166
Copyhold—Power of sale	69
Executors 105,	106
Debts—Devise of estate charged with payment of debts............27,	128
Declaration statutory—By a vendor	146
As to death and identity of a party............................75,	98
Distringas—Inquiry as to distringas on stock 142,	144
Or judge's charging order	155
To be placed on stock after purchase or mortgage..........143,	156
Estate tail in freehold, barred by feoffment and fine, where tenant in tail seized of immediate reversion in fee	6
Estate tail (equitable) in copyhold barred by deed...............103,	166
Estate tail—When protector does not concur........................37,	133
Executor—Sale of leasehold by non-proving executor where trusts declared of leasehold...148,	149
General observations	171
Heir-at-law under old law of inheritance........................136,	153

	PAGE
Heir-at-law under new law of inheritance	153
Inquiry of Trustees 143, 156,	164
Form of letter	144
Inquiry of Chief Accountant of Bank of England 142,	155
Form of letter	144
Judge's charging order—Inquiry as to 155,	175
Leasehold—As to succession duty on sale by administrator......122,	125
Mortgagee—Executors of deceased mortgagee to concur in conveyance	116
Notice of assignment to be given to trustees 143,	165
Form of notice	146
Form of notice of mortgage of policy to directors	63
Observations, general	171
Protector to concur in deed of disentail	133
Recovery—Where no entry of proceedings, or exemplification of recovery can be found......30,	130
Registry—As to leasehold 159,	170
Of will	17
Of letters of administration	122
Searches—as to freeholds...........113, 115, 131, 134, 135	162
As to copyholds 120	139
As to leaseholds 149, 168	169
As to personalty..........143, 156	164
Statutory declaration—*See* Declaration 75, 98,	146
Succession duty, on leasehold, not payable on sale by administrator...	122
Opinion as to such duty	125
Payable on death of annuitant 115,	141
On death of tenant for life	155
To be commuted for when tenant for life, or annuitant, living, 160,	170
Transfer of railway debentures	99
Of railway mortgage bonds	99
Trusts of leasehold—Where sale by executor 148,	149

PART I.

ABSTRACTS OF TITLE:

FREEHOLD.
COPYHOLD.
LEASEHOLD FOR YEARS.
PERSONALTY.

No. 1.

FREEHOLD TITLE.—Abstract of the Title of Peter Garford and Robert Thomas Garford, Esqrs., to a Freehold messuage, farm, and estate, called Melton Farm, situate in the parish of A——, in the county of B——.

Probate copy will of Percival Garford, of, &c., whereby (*inter alia*) said testator gave to his sister Catherine Garford during her life one annuity or yearly rent charge of £300, the same to be paid by equal half-yearly payments in every year, and the first half-yearly payment to be made on the expiration of six calendar months after testator's decease, with a proportionate part for less than six months.

1820,
June 28th.

And said testator charged all and singular his freehold and real estates with the payment of the said annuity.

And the testator empowered the said Catherine Garford by distress, and also by entry upon and perception of the rents and profits of testator's said real estate so charged as aforesaid, to recover payment of the said annuity when in arrear for 30 days, with all consequential costs and expenses.

And subject and charged as aforesaid, the said testator gave and devised all that his messuage, farm,

B

ABSTRACT No. 1.

and estate called Melton Farm, situate in the parish of A—— in the county of B——, then in his own occupation, and containing 470 acres or thereabouts,

To the uses following (that is to say)—
To the use of testator's daughter Maria Garford and the heirs of her body. . . . . remainder.
To the use of the testator's daughter Selina Garford and the heirs of her body . . . . . . remainder.
As to one moiety or half part of said messuage, farm, and estate.
To the use of testator's nephew Peter Garford and his heirs,; but in case the said Peter Garford should die without issue, then
To the use of the said testator's sister, Catherine Garford, and her heirs.
And as to the other moiety of the said messuage, farm, and estate,
To the use of said testator's nephew, Robert Thomas Garford, for his life; and in case he should die without issue, then to the use of said Catherine Garford and her heirs.

Signed by said testator, Percival Garford, and attested by three witnesses.

1826,
November 4th.   Said Percival Garford died.

1826,   Said will proved by said Maria Garford, the executrix,
December 9th. in the Consistory Court of the Bishop of L——.

1830,   Said Maria Garford intermarried with Robert Charlton
May 17th. at the parish church of M——.

The only issue of this marriage was a son, Joseph
1844,   Charlton, who was born on 24th January, 1836.
October 3rd.   Said Joseph Charlton died.

1840,   Said Selina Garford intermarried with Charles Turner
February 23rd. at the parish church of P——.

There was no issue of this marriage.
1858,   Said Selina Turner died without having had issue,
June 9th. and leaving her husband surviving.

Said Charles Turner is living.

1864,   Said Maria Charlton died without leaving any issue
Septem. 26th. her surviving.

Said Robert Charlton is living.
1869,   Said Catherine Garford, the annuitant, died.
April 24th.   Peter Garford and Robert Thomas Garford are both living, and have contracted to sell the estate.

No. 2.

FREEHOLD.—Abstract of the Title of Mr. Benjamin Goodwin to a Freehold estate called Dairy Farm, situate in the parish of D——, in the county of M——.

1810.
July 14th and 15th.

Indentures of lease and release of these dates by the release made between Robert Charles Corbet, of   , in the county of   , Esq., of the 1st part, Arthur Vallotton, of   , Esq., of 2nd part, and Peter Pinder, of   , Gentleman, of 3rd part,

> After reciting that said Robert Charles Corbet had contracted and agreed with said Arthur Vallotton for sale to him of the messuage, lands, and hereditaments thereinafter described and intended to be thereby granted and released, and the inheritance thereof in fee simple in possession, free from all encumbrances, at or for the price or sum of £3,000.

It is by abstracting indenture of release witnessed that, in consideration of £3,000 paid by said Arthur Vallotton to said Robert Charles Corbet, at or before, &c., the receipt, &c., said Robert Charles Corbet did grant, release, and confirm unto said Arthur Vallotton (in his actual possession then being, &c.) and his heirs—

> All that messuage, tenement, and farm house, with the yards, gardens, orchard, barns, stables, and outbuildings thereunto adjoining and belonging and occupied and enjoyed therewith;
> And also the several closes, fields, and inclosures of arable, meadow, and pasture land occupied and enjoyed with the said messuage and farm house, and called or known by the several names and containing by estimation the several quantities mentioned and specified in the schedule written under or annexed to the now abstracting indenture, and containing in the whole by estimate 270 acres, and as the same premises were formerly in the occupation of Thomas Plant and then of said Robert Charles Corbet;
> All which messuage, lands, and premises were situate and being in the parish of D——, in the county of M——, and were known by the name of the Dairy Farm:

ABSTRACT No. 2.

Together, &c., and the reversion, &c., and all estate, &c.,

To hold said messuage, lands, and hereditaments unto said Arthur Vallotton and his heirs,

To such uses, upon and for such trusts, and subject to such powers, provisoes, declarations, and agreements as said Arthur Vallotton, by any deed or deeds to be duly executed by him, should from time to time, or at any time, direct, limit, or appoint ; and in default of and until such appointment, and so far as any such direction, limitation, or appointment should not extend ;

To the use of said Arthur Vallotton and his assigns during his life, without impeachment of waste, with a limitation ;

To the use of said Peter Pinder, his executors and administrators, during the life of said Arthur Vallotton nevertheless, in trust for said Arthur Vallotton and his assigns ; . . . remainder ;

"Heirs" word of Limitation.

To use of the heirs of said Arthur Vallotton for ever.

Covenants by said Robert Charles Corbet :
That he was lawfully seized.
Had power to convey.
For peaceable possession.
Freedom from incumbrances.
And for further assurance, schedule of parcels to be set out.

Executed by said Robert Charles Corbet, and attested.

Receipt for £3,000 endorsed, signed by said R. C. Corbet, and witnessed.

1824, November 19th

Probate copy will of said Arthur Vallotton of this date, whereby said testator gave and devised his freehold farm called Dairy Farm, situate in the parish of D——, and all other his freehold estates in the county of M——, with their appurtenances—

To the following uses (that is to say) :

To use of testator's nephew, Gabriel Vallotton, and his assigns, during his life ; and after his decease,

ABSTRACT No. 2.

To the use of the heirs of the body of said Gabriel Vallotton; and for default of such issue, "Heirs of body" words of Limitation.
To the use of said testator's niece, Clara Vallotton, and the heirs of her body; and, for default of such issue, Limitation.
To the use of the heirs of said Gabriel Vallotton for ever. Limitation.

    Signed by said Arthur Vallotton,
    and attested by three witnesses.

Said Arthur Vallotton died and was buried at the parish of D——, in county of M——.   1825, June 27th.
Said will proved in Exchequer Court of York.   1825, October 4th.
Said Clara Vallotton died without issue, an infant (aged 17), and unmarried.   1826, May 9th.

By indenture of feoffment of this date, made between said Gabriel Vallotton, of one part, and Robert Limond, of , in county of , of second part, and John Thorburn, of , of third part,   1828, January 2nd.

> Reciting said abstracted will of said Arthur Vallotton, and his death on 27th June, 1825, and proof of his will.
> And reciting that said Clara Vallotton died on 9th May, 1826, an infant, and unmarried, and that she was buried at , in the county of , on 16th May, 1826.
> And reciting that said Gabriel Vallotton had no issue, and was a bachelor and unmarried.
> And reciting that said Gabriel Vallotton had contracted with said Robert Limond for absolute sale to him of said messuage, farm, and premises, called Dairy Farm, and the inheritance thereof in fee simple in possession, free from incumbrances, for £4,000,

It is by abstracting indenture witnessed, that in consideration of £4,000 to said Gabriel Vallotton paid by said Robert Limond at or before, &c., the receipt, &c., said Gabriel Vallotton did grant, enfeoff, and confirm unto said Robert Limond and his heirs—

> All said messuage, farm, and lands, hereinbefore described, and comprised in said abstracted indentures of 14th and 15th July, 1810, by a similar description.

6   ABSTRACT No. 2.

To hold same unto said Robert Limond and his heirs.
To use of said Robert Limond and John Thorburn, and the heirs and assigns of said Robert Limond, for ever, nevertheless as to the estate and interest of said John Thorburn in said premises. In trust for said Robert Limond, his heirs and assigns.

Covenant by said Gabriel Vallotton to levy a fine sur conuzance de droit come ceo, &c., of said premises.

Declaration that such fine should enure. To uses thereinbefore declared of said premises.

Covenants by said Gabriel Vallotton:
That he was lawfully seized.
Had good right to convey.
For peaceable possession.
Freedom from incumbrances.
And for further assurance.

Executed by said Gabriel Vallotton, and attested.

Receipt for £4,000 endorsed, signed by said Gabriel Vallotton, and witnessed.

Livery of seizin endorsed.

1828,
Hilary Term.

Chirograph indentures of fine, wherein said Robert Limond was Plaintiff and said Gabriel Vallotton was Deforceant, of
Two messuages, 2 cottages, 2 barns, 2 stables, 2 gardens, 2 orchards, 500 acres of land, 300 acres of pasture, 100 acres of wood and common of pasture and turbary in the parish of D——, in the county of M——.

Proclamations endorsed.

1842,
March 15th.

Legal Estate in Trustees.

Probate copy will of said Robert Limond, whereby (*inter alia*) he gave and devised his farm, called Dairy Farm, situate in D——, and all other his real and freehold estates whatsoever, unto and to the use of his friends Charles Porter and Abraham Walton, their heirs and assigns, for ever, upon the following trusts (that is to say) :—

In trust for testator's son Christopher Limond and
his assigns during his life . . . . remainder.
In trust for the first and every other the son and sons "Son and sons"
of said Christopher Limond severally and successively words of Purchase.
one after another, and the heirs male of the body and
bodies of such son and sons lawfully issuing . remainder.
In trust for the right heirs of said Christopher "Heirs" word
Limond for ever. of Limitation.

      Signed by said Robert Limond,
      and attested by two witnesses.

Said Robert Limond died.   1850, November 4th.
Said will proved in Prerogative Court of York.   1850, December 17th.

Indenture of this date made between said Christopher   1864,
Limond of one part, and Benjamin Goodwin of other   June 23rd.
part,
 Reciting said abstracted will of said Robert Limond.
 And reciting that said Christopher Limond had
  no issue.
 And reciting that said Christopher Limond had
  contracted and agreed with said Benjamin Goodwin for the absolute sale to him of said messuage, farm, and lands, called Dairy Farm, and the inheritance thereof in fee simple in possession, for the sum of £5,600.

It is by abstracting indenture witnessed that in consideration of £5,600, by said Benjamin Goodwin paid to said Christopher Limond at or before execution, &c., the receipt, &c., said Christopher Limond did grant, convey, and confirm unto said Benjamin Goodwin and his heirs—
 Said messuage, farm, and lands, called Dairy Farm, comprised in and conveyed by said abstracted indenture of 2nd January, 1828, by a similar description. Together, &c., and all estate, &c.

To hold same premises unto and
To the use of said Benjamin Goodwin, his heirs and "Heirs" word
assigns for ever. of Limitation.

Covenants by said Christopher Limond :
 That he was lawfully seized.
 Had power to convey.

For peaceable possession.
Free from incumbrances.
And further assurance.

Executed by said Christopher Limond, and attested.

Receipt for £5,600 endorsed, signed by said Christopher Limond, and witnessed.

1868,
May 30th.
Said Christopher Limond died a bachelor without having had any issue, and was buried at

1870,
February 20th.
Indenture of this date made between said Benjamin Goodwin of one part, and Thomas Bryan and James Ludlam of other part.

It is witnessed that in consideration of £2,000 to said Benjamin Goodwin paid by said Thomas Bryan and James Ludlam, the receipt, &c., said Benjamin Goodwin did grant and confirm to said Bryan and Ludlam and their heirs—

Said messuage, farm, and lands, before described.

Together, &c., and all estate, &c.

To hold same unto and to use of said Thomas Bryan and James Ludlam, their heirs and assigns, for ever.

Proviso for redemption and reconveyance of said premises, on payment by said Benjamin Goodwin, his heirs, executors, administrators, or assigns, to said Thomas Bryan and James Ludlam, their executors, administrators, or assigns, of £2,000, on 20th August then next.

Usual mortgage covenants.

Executed by said Benjamin Goodwin, and attested.

Receipt for £2,000 endorsed, signed by said Benjamin Goodwin, and witnessed.

1870,
December 7th.
Said Thomas Bryan died and was buried at

No. 3.

COPYHOLD TITLE.—Abstract of the Title of George
    Penistan, Esq., and mortgagee, to a Copyhold
    messuage and estate, called Elm Place, situate in
    the parish of D——, and held of the manor of
    D——, in the county of S——.

Manor of D——, in the county of S——.

At a General Court Baron, held in and for said manor, Jacob Penistan, of   , in the county of S——, Esq., was admitted tenant, on the surrender of Mary Best, widow, to   *1802, May 18th.*

    All that customary messuage or tenement, and all
    those 40 acres of land customary and heritable,
    called Elm Place, held of said manor by copy of
    Court Roll, and situate at ——, in the parish of
    D——, and within said manor,

To hold same to said Jacob Penistan, his heirs and assigns, for ever, at the will of the lord, according to the custom of said manor, by the yearly rent of £17 4s. suit of Court customs and services therefore due and of right accustomed, and he gave to the lord for a fine as appears in the margin, and his fealty was respited.

Examined by
A—— B——,
Steward.

Same Court.

    Said Jacob Penistan surrendered all his copyhold
    messuages, lands, and tenements holden of said
    manor,
To the use of his last will and testament.

Probate copy will of said Jacob Penistan, whereby (*inter alia*) said testator devised   *1830, October 9th.*

    This copyhold messuage and estate, called Elm
    Place, then in his own occupation, situate in the
    manor and parish of D——, in the county of
    S——, and all his personal estate and effects,

To his wife Judith Penistan during her life; and after her death

To testator's daughter, Maria Penistan, her heirs, executors, administrators, and assigns.

And said testator further devised and directed that in case his said daughter Maria Penistan should die in the lifetime of testator's said wife Judith, then the property thereby devised and given to his said daughter Maria should be sold by his executors, and that the money arising from the sale thereof should be equally divided between the children of testator's deceased son Robert Penistan, or the survivors or survivor of them.

And said testator appointed his brothers William Penistan and Edward Penistan executors of his said will.

N.B.—This will is not attested by any witness.

1842,
March 4th.   Said Jacob Penistan died, leaving his wife Judith and his daughter Maria Penistan both living.

1842,
June 13th.   Said will proved by said executors in Consistory Court of Bishop of L——.

1842,
September 19th   At a General Court Baron held in and for said manor of D——,

At this Court the homage presented

That said Jacob Penistan, late a customary tenant of said manor, who held to him and his heirs of the lord of the said manor

  All that customary messuage or tenement, and
    40 acres of land customary, called Elm Place,
    situate in   quarter within said manor,
died on 4th March, 1842, seized of said copyhold premises,

And setting out said will of said Jacob Penistan.

And the homage further presented that said Judith Penistan, the widow of said testator, died on 30th August then last, leaving said Maria Penistan (testator's daughter) surviving.

At this Court came said Maria Penistan by William Jones, her attorney, and prayed to be admitted tenant of the lord to the said copyhold premises so devised to her as aforesaid, to whom the lord of said manor by said steward delivered seizin thereof by the rod, to hold said premises unto said Maria Penistan, her heirs and assigns, of the lord, according to the tenor of said will,

ABSTRACT No. 3.

and according to the custom of said manor, at the yearly rent, customs, and services therefore due, and of right accustomed.

And she gave to the lord for a fine as much as appear in the margin, and was therefore admitted tenant in form aforesaid, and her fealty was respited.

Examined by
A—— B——,
Steward.

By indenture of this date made between said Maria Penistan of one part, and Robert Inwood, of Esq., of other part,   1860, October 27th.

    Reciting (*inter alia*) said last abstracted admission, and reciting agreement for loan of £2,000 by said Robert Inwood to said Maria Penistan,

It is witnessed that in consideration of £2,000 by said Robert Inwood paid to said Maria Penistan (the receipt, &c.) said Maria Penistan did grant and convey to said Robert Inwood and his heirs

    Certain freehold hereditaments in abstracting indenture described;

    To hold same unto and to the use of said Robert Inwood, his heirs and assigns, for ever,

    Subject to a proviso in abstracting indenture contained for redemption and reconveyance of said premises on payment by said Maria Penistan, her heirs, executors, administrators, or assigns, to said Robert Inwood, his executors, administrators, or assigns, of £2,000, and interest at £5 per centum per annum, on 27th October, 1861.

Usual mortgage covenant for payment of principal and interest.

And it was by abstracting indenture further witnessed that for consideration aforesaid, said Maria Penistan did covenant with said Robert Inwood that said M. Penistan or her heirs, and all other necessary parties, would at her or their costs at or before next General Court to be holden in and for said manor of D——, surrender into the hands of lord of said manor, to the use of said Robert Inwood, his heirs and assigns,

All said copyhold or customary messuage, lands, and hereditaments to which said Maria Penistan was admitted tenant at said court, held on 19th September, 1842, as aforesaid.

And all houses, commons, &c.

To hold said copyhold premises unto said Robert Inwood and his heirs at the will of the lord, according to custom of said manor, by the rents, &c.

Subject to a proviso for redemption of said premises similar to proviso thereinbefore contained for redemption of said freehold premises.

Usual mortgage covenants for title.

Power of sale.

Executed by said Maria Penistan, and attested.

Receipt for £2,000 endorsed, signed, by said Maria Penistan, and witnessed.

1870,
June 17th.

The Manor of D——, } Conditional Surrender out of
in the county of S——.   } Court and out of Manor.*

Be it remembered that on the 17th day of June, 1870, Maria Penistan, of &c., spinster, one of the customary tenants of the said manor, came before A. B., of, &c., Gentleman (deputy-steward of the said manor for this turn only), at No.   Lincoln's Inn New Square, in the county of Middlesex, and, in pursuance of and conformably to a covenant for that purpose made and entered into by the said Maria Penistan in and by a certain indenture of mortgage, bearing date the 27th day of October, 1860, expressed to be made between the said Maria Penistan of the one part, and Robert Inwood, of   , in the county of   , Esq., of the other part, and in consideration of the sum of £2,000 in such indenture expressed to be paid by the said Robert Inwood to the said Maria Penistan, as therein mentioned (and which sum of £2,000 now remains due on the security of the said indenture), Did out of court

---

* N.B.—This Surrender is set out fully. Under the 78 Sec. of 4 & 5 Vic., c. 35, a Surrender may now be taken out of court, and out of the manor, by any person authorised by the steward of the manor, without any power of attorney from the steward. It is usual to pay the ordinary fees to the steward, as if the Surrender were taken by him.

(to wit), at No.   Lincoln's Inn New Square, aforesaid, surrender into the hands of the lord of the said manor by the hands and acceptance of the said deputy-steward by the rod, and according to the custom of the said manor,

    All that copyhold or customary messuage or tenement, and all those 40 acres of land, customary and other hereditaments, called Elm Place, parcel and held of the said manor of D———, by copy of Court Roll, and all other the copyhold hereditaments to which the said Maria Penistan was admitted tenant at a General Court held in and for said manor on the 19th day of September, 1842, with the rights, members, and appurtenances to said copyhold premises belonging or appertaining, and all the estate, right, title, interest, inheritance, use, trust, property, claim, and demand whatsoever, both at law and in equity, of the said Maria Penistan, into and out of the said copyhold or customary hereditaments and premises and every part thereof,

To the use of the said Robert Inwood, his heirs and assigns, for ever, to be held of the lord according to the custom of the said manor, by the rents, fines, and services therefore due, and of right accustomed;

    Subject to this proviso or condition, that if the said Maria Penistan, her heirs, executors, administrators, or assigns, do and shall, on the 27th day of October next, pay or cause to be paid to the said Robert Inwood, his executors, administrators, or assigns, the said principal sum of £2,000 (now remaining due on the security of the said indenture of mortgage of the 27th day of October, 1860), and all interest then due for the same, then this surrender is to be void and of no effect, otherwise the same shall remain in full force and virtue.

                (Signed)   Maria Penistan.

This surrender was taken and accepted the day and year first above written, by me,

                A——— B———,
           Deputy-steward of the said Manor.
               for this turn only.

1871, March 27th.	Said Maria Penistan died intestate, leaving George Penistan, her youngest brother and heir according to the custom of said manor. By the custom of the manor, the descent is to the youngest son or youngest brother of the tenant dying seized.

No. 4.

LEASEHOLD FOR YEARS.—Abstract of the Title of the administratrix of Mr. Charles Seton, and his mortgagee, to two Leasehold houses and gardens, being Nos. 1 and 2, Victoria Terrace,
Road, in the parish of St.   , in the county of Middlesex.

1850, April 3rd.	By indenture of lease of this date, made between William Thompson, of , in the county of , Esquire, of the one part, and Samuel Allen, of , in the county of , of the other part,

It is witnessed that, in consideration of the expense incurred and sustained by said Samuel Allen in building the messuages and buildings thereby demised, and in consideration of the rents and covenants thereinafter reserved and continued, said William Thompson did demise and lease to said Samuel Allen—

> All that piece of land or ground situate on the west side of   Road, in the parish of   , in the county of Middlesex, containing the several dimensions, and abutting as is shewn in the plan drawn in margin of abstracting indenture, together with the two several messuages or tenements thereon erected and built fronting said road, and then known as Nos. 1 and 2, Victoria Terrace,
> Road, aforesaid,

To hold unto said Samuel Allen, his executors, administrators, and assigns, from 24th March then last for the term of 99 years,

> Yielding and paying unto said William Thompson,

his heirs and assigns, for each of said messuages and the site thereof, and the garden and appurtenances thereto, the yearly rent of £10, payable quarterly on the usual quarterly days, clear of all deductions (except for landlord's property tax).

Covenants by said Samuel Allen : —

To pay said rents. —

To pay sewers rate and all taxes and rates. —

To finish each messuage fit for habitation, and to expend thereon in the whole £800 at least on each messuage.

To repair, insure, &c., within 3 calendar months after the execution of any assignment or underlease of either of said messuages for any term longer than 21 years, to give notice in writing to lessor or his solicitor or agent, and to pay with such notice a fee of 10s. 6d. for registering same.

Proviso for re-entry on nonpayment of rent or breach of covenants.

Declaration and agreement that no default in payment of rent reserved for or in the performance of any of the covenants in conditions and agreements applicable to only one of said two several messuages or tenements and the appurtenances thereto belonging should be or occasion a forfeiture of the other of said messuages or tenements and the appurtenances thereto belonging. It being expressly intended and agreed by parties to the now abstracting indenture, that each of the said messuages and the tenant or tenants thereof for time being should be liable only to the payment of the rent reserved for each such messuage and premises, and the observance and performance of the covenants, conditions, and agreements which related to and were to be observed and performed in respect of the same messuage and premises.

Executed by both parties and attested.

Registered in Middlesex 30th April, 1850, Book   , No. .

Said Samuel Allen died intestate.

1854, March 8th.

ABSTRACT No. 4.

1854,
April 17th.
Letters of administration of the goods, chattels, and personal estate of said Samuel Allen were granted to Thomas Allen, his father and only next of kin, by the Prerogative Court of the Archbishop of Canterbury.

1864.
May 3rd.
By indenture of this date made between said Thomas Allen of one part and Walter Jones, of   , of other part,

 After reciting said abstracted lease, the death of said Samuel Allen intestate, and said letters of administration,

It is witnessed that in consideration of £1,500 to said Thomas Allen (as such administrator as aforesaid) paid by said Walter Jones, the receipt, &c., said Thomas Allen (as such administrator as aforesaid) did grant, assign, and confirm to said Walter Jones—

 All said piece of ground and said two messuages or tenements, and all other the premises comprised in and demised by said lease, with the appurtenances, and all estate, &c.,

To hold same premises to said Walter Jones, his executors, administrators, and assigns, during all then residue of said term of 99 years created by said lease,

 At and subject to payment of rents and performance of covenants reserved and contained by and in said abstracted indenture of lease.

Covenant by said Thomas Allen that he had not incumbered; covenant by said Walter Jones for payment of rent and performance of covenants.

   Executed by both parties and attested.

   Receipt for £1,500 endorsed, signed by Thomas Allen, and witnessed.

Registered in Middlesex 10th May, 1864, Book   , No.   .

1868,
September 23rd
Said Walter Jones died intestate.

1868,
November 15th
Letters of administration of the personal estate of said Walter Jones were granted to Mary Jones, his widow, by Her Majesty's Court of Probate at the Principal Registry.

1869,
January 4th.
By indenture of this date made between said Mary

ABSTRACT No. 4.

Jones, of   , widow, of the one part, and Charles Seton, of   , in the county of Middlesex, of the other part,

After reciting said abstracted indenture of lease of 3rd April, 1850,

And reciting said death of said Samuel Allen and the letters of administration granted to Thomas Allen,

And reciting said abstracted indenture of 3rd May, 1864,

And reciting death of said Walter Jones intestate, and said last abstracted letters of administration,

And reciting that said Mary Jones had contracted with said Charles Seton for sale to him of said leasehold messuages for £2,000,

It is by abstracting indenture witnessed that in consideration of £2,000 paid to said Mary Jones (as such administratrix as aforesaid) by said Charles Seton, the receipt, &c., said Mary Jones (as such administratrix as aforesaid), did grant and assign to said Charles Seton, his executors, administrators, and assigns—

The said two several messuages or tenements, piece of ground, and all other the premises comprised in and demised by said abstracted indenture of lease of 3rd April, 1850, with the appurtenances, and all the estate, term of years, &c., of said Mary Jones (as such administratrix as aforesaid),

To hold same to said Charles Seton, his executors, administrators, and assigns, for all then residue of said term of 99 years, created by said abstracted lease,

At and under the rents and covenants reserved and contained by and in said abstracted indenture of lease, and thenceforth on part of lessee or assignee to be paid and performed.

Covenant by said Mary Jones, that she had not encumbered.

Covenant by said Charles Seton, to pay rents and perform covenants.

   Executed by said Mary Jones and Charles Seton, and attested.

   Receipt for £2,000 indorsed, signed by said Mary Jones, and witnessed.

   Registered in Middlesex, 15th January, 1869, Book   , No.   .

1870,
March 17th.

Indenture of mortgage of this date, made between said Charles Seton, of one part, and Thomas Phillips, of   , of other part;

 Reciting said abstracted indenture of lease of 3rd April, 1850.

 And reciting that under and by virtue of divers mesne assignments and acts in law, and ultimately by last abstracted indenture of 4th January, 1869, said leasehold messuages and premises comprised in said lease had become vested in said Charles Seton during residue of said term of 99 years.

 And reciting that said Charles Seton had requested said Thomas Phillips to lend to him the sum of £1,000, which he had agreed to do upon having the repayment thereof with interest after the rate of £   per centum per annum secured to him in manner thereinafter expressed.

It is by abstracting indenture witnessed that in consideration of the sum of £1,000 to said Charles Seton by said Phillips, on or before execution, &c., the receipt, &c., said Charles Seton did covenant with said Phillips to pay him on 17th September then next the sum of £1,000, with interest for same after the rate of £   per centum per annum without any deduction (except for property tax on interest), and covenant to pay further interest.

And it was by abstracting indenture further witnessed that for consideration aforesaid, said Charles Seton did grant and demise unto said Thomas Phillips, his executors, administrators, and assigns—

 The said piece of ground and the two messuages or tenements and all other the premises comprised in and demised by the said recited indenture of lease of 3rd April, 1850; and all and singular the tenant's fixtures in and about the premises;

---

* N.B.—In preparing a mortgage of leasehold property, it is important expressly to include the tenant's fixtures, as, in some cases, if the mortgagor be in the actual possession of the property, he may claim the right to remove the fixtures; and dispute the right of the mortgagee to sell the fixtures under the power of sale. But there can be no doubt that, as between mortgagor and mortgagee, the fixtures pass with the property mortgaged, whether it be leasehold or freehold, as appears from the following judgment of the Court of Exchequer in 1868:—

"The term 'Fixture' is an ambiguous one. This is a case between

To hold same to said Thomas Phillips, his executors, administrators, and assigns, for all the residue of said term of 99 years created by said lease, except the last day of said term.

Proviso for redemption of said premises on payment by said Charles Seton, his heirs, executors, administrators, or assigns, to said Thomas Phillips, his executors, administrators, or assigns, of £1,000, with interest after rate of £   per centum per annum, on 17th September then next.

Usual mortgage covenants.

Power of sale. [To be set out at length, and power to give receipts.]

   Executed by said Charles Seton, and attested.

   Receipt for £1,000 indorsed, signed by said Charles Seton, and witnessed.

   Registered in Middlesex, 25th March, 1870, Book   , No.   .

Said Charles Seton died intestate.   1870, May 4th.

Letters of administration of the personal estate of said Charles Seton, granted to Catherine Seton, his widow and relict, by Her Majesty's Court of Probate, at the Principal Registry.   1870, June 14th.

This is an ordinary leasehold title.

After perusing the foregoing abstract (leasehold for years), the student will assume that the leasehold property (including the tenant's fixtures) has been sold by auction by the administratrix of Charles Seton.

That the conditions of sale stipulate—

"Mortgagor and Mortgagee, and no authority can be cited to show that "a Mortgagor is entitled to remove trade or other fixtures.
  "A Mortgage is a security for a debt, and it is not unreasonable, if a "fixture be annexed to Land at the time of a Mortgage, or if the Mortgagor "in possession afterwards annexes a fixture to it, that the fixtures shall be "deemed an additional security for the debt, whether it be a trade fixture "or a fixture of any other kind.—Per Kelly C. B. Climie *v*, Wood, 3 L. R. "(Exchequer) 260."

That the title of the lessor shall not be called for, investigated, or objected to;

That all office copies, certificates, and declarations, required by the purchaser, shall be furnished at his expense;

That the vendor shall only covenant that she has not encumbered;

And the other usual conditions.

The student will then consider what requisitions should be prepared, and what information required, on the part of the purchaser.

No. 5.

FREEHOLD.—Abstract of the Title of Mary Ann Appleton to a Freehold mansion and estate, situate in the parish of   , in the county of

1832,
Jan. 8th & 9th. By indentures of lease and release, of these dates respectively, made between Benjamin Stratton, of   ,   , Esquire, of one part, and Christopher Combe, of   , of other part.

It is by abstracting indenture of release witnessed that in consideration of £3,000, by said Christopher Combe paid to said Benjamin Stratton, the receipt, &c., said Benjamin Stratton did grant, release, and confirm unto said Christopher Combe (in his actual possession, &c.) and his heirs—

> All that messuage, mansion house, or tenement, called Temple House, and the coach-house, stables, out-buildings, gardens, orchard, and ground, held and occupied therewith, containing in the whole 20 acres, all which messuage and premises were situate and being in the parish of   in the county of   .
> and were bounded on the   by the high road leading from   to   to   ,
> and on the   by the River N——,

and which mansion house and premises were then in the occupation of the said Benjamin Stratton.

Together, &c., reversion, &c., estate, &c.

To hold said messuage, lands, and premises unto and
To the use of said Christopher Combe, his heirs and assigns for ever, subject to proviso for redemption thereinafter contained.

Proviso for redemption and reconveyance of said hereditaments, on payment, by said Benjamin Stratton, his heirs, executors, administrators, or assigns, to said Christopher Combe, his executors, administrators, or assigns, of £3,000, with interest in the meantime after the rate of £5 per cent. per annum, on 9th July then next ensuing.

Usual mortgage covenants.

> Lease and release executed by said Benjamin Stratton, and attested.
>
> Receipt for £3,000 endorsed on release, signed by said Benjamin Stratton, and witnessed.

By indentures of lease and release of these dates respectively, made between said Benjamin Stratton, of one part, and Mary Carter, of, &c., of other part, — **1836, October 23rd & 24th.**

It is by abstracting indenture of release witnessed, that in consideration of £2,000 to said Benjamin Stratton paid by said Mary Carter, said Benjamin Stratton did grant, release, and confirm unto said Mary Carter (in her actual possession, &c.) and her heirs—

> Said mansion house, ground, and premises, comprised in and conveyed by last abstracted indenture by a similar description.

Together, &c., reversion, &c., estate, &c.

To hold said premises unto and
To the use of said Mary Carter, her heirs and assigns, for ever, subject to proviso for redemption thereinafter contained.

Usual mortgage covenants.

Proviso for redemption of said premises on payment by said Benjamin Stratton, his heirs, executors, administrators, or assigns, to said Mary Carter, her executors, administrators, or assigns, of £2,000, with interest at £5 per cent., on 24th of April then next.

Executed by Benjamin Stratton, and witnessed.

Receipt for £2,000 endorsed on release, signed by said Benjamin Stratton, and witnessed.

1840, June 10th.

By a Decree made by the High Court of Chancery, by His Honour the Master of the Rolls, on the hearing of a Cause wherein the said Christopher Combe was Plaintiff, and the said Benjamin Stratton and Mary Carter and others were Defendants,

It was ordered that it should be referred to the Master of the said Court in rotation, to compute what was due to the Plaintiff for principal and interest on his mortgage securities in the pleadings in that Cause mentioned, and to tax the costs, charges, and expenses, incurred in respect of the same, inclusive of the costs of the said suit; and that the said Master should distinguish in respect of which estate such costs, charges, and expenses were incurred. And it was ordered that the said Master should take an account of the rents and profits of the said mortgaged premises come to the hands of the said Plaintiff, or to the hands of any other person or persons, by his order or for his use, or which without his wilful default might have been received. And it was ordered that what should be found to have been received on the said account of rents and profits should be deducted from what should be found due to the Plaintiff for such principal, interest, and costs; and that the said Master should state the amount of the balance due to said Plaintiff on such accounts.

And it was ordered that in case the said Master should think fit, he should cause an advertisement to be published in the *London Gazette*, and such other papers as he should think fit, for the creditors under the said indentures to come in and prove their debts, and he was to fix a peremptory day for that purpose; and such of the said creditors as should not come in to prove their debts by the time so to be appointed, were to be excluded from the benefit of the said reciting decree;

That the reciting decree should be without prejudice to the question whether said Plaintiff was or was not entitled to a decree of foreclosure of said mortgaged premises, and for the better taking such accounts and discovery of the matters aforesaid, all parties were to produce before said Master, upon oath, all deeds, books, papers, and writings, in their custody, or power relating thereto, and were to be examined upon interrogatories, as the said Master should direct, who, in taking said accounts, was to make to all parties all just allowances; and the Master was to be at liberty to state any circumstances specially as he should think fit.

Consideration of further* directions reserved until after report.

Liberty to apply.

Duly passed and entered.

By his report of this date, made in the said Cause, the Master, A——— B———, Esq., found (*inter alia*) the several before abstracted indentures of mortgage. And he found that in the month of   , 18 , said Plaintiff, Christopher Combe, entered into possession and the receipt of the rents and profits of the said mortgaged premises, comprised in his mortgage securities, and had continued in such possession up to that present time.

And the said Master (*inter alia*) found that the principal sums of £   and £   , making together £   , were the total amount of principal money secured by the said mortgage securities.

And the said Master found (*inter alia*) that the sum of £   was then due to the said Plaintiff for principal, interest, and costs.

Signed and filed the
17th August, 1848.

1848,
June 17th.

The said Master's report was absolutely confirmed by an order of the said Court of this date.

1848,
November 8th.

1849,
March 3rd.

By an order made, on the said Cause coming on to be heard, for further directions, and on the petition of the said Christopher Combe, the Court did, by consent, order that the mortgaged premises in the pleadings mentioned should be sold, with the approbation of the Master, to the best purchaser or purchasers that could be got, for the same to be allowed of by the said Master, and all proper practices were to join therein as the said Master should direct.

And it was ordered that any of the parties should be at liberty to bid at such sale.

And it was ordered [directions as to reserved biddings].

And it was ordered that the purchase-money should be paid into the Bank, with the privity of the Accountant-General of the said Court, to the credit of the first-mentioned Cause.

And it was ordered, &c. [directions as to taxing costs, computing interest, &c.]

And the Court did declare the Plaintiff to be entitled to be paid, in the first place and in priority, the amount of what should be reported due to him for principal, interest, and costs, charges and expenses, and costs of suit.

Consideration of all further directions and the costs of the other defendants reserved until after the Master should have made his report.

Liberty for all parties to apply to the Court as there should be occasion.

Passed and entered.

1849,
May 23rd.

Order made in the said Causes. Whereby, after stating that by an order dated the 4th May, 1849, it was ordered that the report made in these Causes by Mr.   , one of the Masters of the said Court, dated the 29th day of April, 1849, whereby Jacob Appleton was allowed the purchaser of the premises in Lot   , part of the estates in question in these Causes, at the sum of £6,000, should stand ratified and confirmed, unless, &c. It was by now abstracting order ordered that the said order should be made absolute.

Passed and entered.

1850,
August 19th.

By indenture of grant and release of this date made between the said Benjamin Stratton, of the first part;

said Christopher Combe (by Peter Wilkinson, his attorney, lawfully authorised in this behalf by a certain power of attorney thereunto annexed), of second part; said Mary Carter, of third part; and Jacob Appleton, of, &c., of fourth part. Reciting the several before-abstracted indentures of mortgage.

And reciting the before-abstracted decree of 10th June, 1840, Master's report of 17th June, 1848, and order of the 3rd March, 1849.

And reciting that in pursuance of the said order, the messuage and other hereditaments thereinafter described, and thereby released, were put up to sale by auction at , with the approbation of the said Master, on the day of , 1849; and that said Jacob Appleton was the highest bidder for the same at such sale, and the purchaser thereof, at the sum of £6,000, and declared to be such purchaser by an order of the said Court dated the 23rd day of May, 1849.

And reciting that the said Jacob Appleton, in obedience to the said order, did on the day of then past pay into the Bank of England, with the privity of the Accountant-General of the Court of Chancery, the sum of £6,000, being the purchase-money aforesaid; and the sum of £ the valuation of the fixtures, and the sum of £ for interest, making together the sum of £6,400, to the credit of the said Cause of *v.* , as appeared by the receipt of J—— R——, one of the cashiers of the Bank of England, and by the certificate of the said Accountant-General.

It is by the abstracting indenture witnessed that in pursuance of and in obedience to the said decree or decretal order, and for the considerations thereinbefore mentioned, the said Benjamin Stratton did grant, bargain, sell, and release, and the said Christopher Combe, by his said attorney, and Mary Carter (according to their respective estates), did release and confirm unto the said Jacob Appleton and his heirs,

> All that the said messuage or mansion house, called or known by the name of Temple House, situate in the parish of , in the county of , and all other the hereditaments and premises comprised in the said first abstracted indenture of mortgage by a similar description.

Together, &c., reversion, &c., all estate, &c.

To hold same, with the appurtenances, unto and to the use of the said Jacob Appleton, his heirs and assigns, for ever. (Freed and absolutely discharged from the said several mortgage securities, and all interest, claims, and demands in respect thereof.)

Covenants by said Christopher Combe and Mary Carter that they had not encumbered.

Covenants for title by said Benjamin Stratton.

Executed by all parties, and attested.

This deed is executed by "Christopher Combe," by Peter Wilkinson, his attorney, as to Combe's execution.

The attestation is "signed, sealed, and delivered by Peter Wilkinson, as the attorney, in the name, and as the act and deed, of the within-named Christopher Combe, in the presence of"

Two witnesses.

1856, May 28th.

The said Jacob Appleton made his will of this date, and thereby, after directing his funeral and testamentary expenses to be paid by his executor,

The testator gave and bequeathed all his property he was possessed of, or might be at the time of his decease, unto his nephew, Richard Appleton, for his own absolute use.

And he appointed his said nephew sole executor of his will.

Signed by said testator, and attested by three witnesses.

1859, December 7th.

Said Jacob Appleton died.

1860, February 24th.

The said will proved by said Richard Appleton at District Registry of B——.

1864,

Decree of dissolution of marriage between Mary Anne Gleppin and Thomas Gleppin.

In Her Majesty's Court for Divorce and Matrimonial Causes.

Before the Right Hon. A—— B——, Knight, Judge

ABSTRACT No. 5.

of Her Majesty's Court of Probate and Judge Ordinary of Her Majesty's Court for Divorce and Matrimonial Causes, sitting in open Court at Westminster.

Gleppin, Gleppin,
Mary Ann. Thomas.

The Judge Ordinary, referring to the decree made in this Cause on the day of , 1863, whereby it was ordered that the marriage had and solemnised on the day of , 1860, at the parish church of , in the county of , between Mary Ann Gleppin, then Mary Ann Appleton, spinster, the petitioner, and Thomas Gleppin, the respondent, should be dissolved by reason of the adultery committed by the respondent, coupled with desertion of his wife without reasonable cause for two years and upwards, unless sufficient cause should be shewn to the Court why the said decree should not be made absolute within six months from the making thereof, and no such cause having been shewn, the Judge Ordinary aforesaid, on motion of counsel for the said petitioner, by his final decree pronounced and declared the said marriage to be dissolved.

1864,
April 9th.

Signed, C—— D——,
       Registrar.

Probate copy will of said Richard Appleton, of this date.

1870,
November 14th.

Whereby (*inter alia*) he directed that all his just debts should be duly paid by his executrix, and he charged all his freehold and copyhold estates with the payment thereof.

And said testator gave and devised

> All his freehold and copyhold and real and personal estates and effects whatsoever and wheresoever, with the appurtenances, unto his sister, the said Mary Ann Appleton, for her own absolute use and benefit.

And he appointed his said sister, Mary Ann Appleton, sole executrix of his said will.

Said Richard Appleton died.

1870,
December 26th.

1871,
May 14th.

Said will proved by said Mary Ann Appleton, single woman (theretofore wife of Thomas Gleppin), the sister of the deceased, at District Registry of

No. 6.

FREEHOLD TITLE.—Abstract of the Title of the Trustee of the Will of Joseph Bettinson, Esquire, to a Freehold mansion and estate, called Ashfield Court, situate in the parish of W———, in the county of D———.

1808,
July 19th.

By indenture of this date, made between Robert Franklyn, of, &c., Esquire, of the 1st part. Edward Franklyn, of, &c., Esq. (the eldest son of the said Robert Franklyn), of the 2nd part, Mary Denton, of, &c., spinster, of the 3rd part, and Charles Charlton and Richard Robinson of, &c., of the 4th part,

After reciting that said Robert Franklyn was then seized to him and his heirs for an estate in fee simple in possession of and in the messuage, lands, and hereditaments thereinafter described, And reciting that a marriage had been agreed upon between said Edward Franklyn and Mary Denton, and that it had been agreed that said hereditaments should be settled in manner thereinafter expressed;

It is by abstracting indenture witnessed that in pursuance of such agreement, and in consideration of said intended marriage, and of the fortune which said Mary Denton would bring to said Edward Franklyn, said Robert Franklyn did for himself, his heirs, executors, and administrators covenant with said Charlton and Robinson, and their heirs, and also with said Edward Franklyn and his heirs. That said Robert Franklyn and his heirs would and should thenceforth stand seized of and in

Covenant to stand seized.

All that messuage, mansion, houses, or tenements, called Ashfield Court, with the coach-house, stables, lawns, gardens, and appurtenances, and the several pieces or parcels of land or ground

ABSTRACT No. 6. 29

adjoining thereto, and occupied therewith, containing altogether by estimation 120 acres, which premises were situate in the parish of W———, in the county of D———, and were then in the occupation of said Robert Franklyn or his tenants, and of and in the rights, members, and appurtenances to said premises belonging or appertaining, to the uses following, (*i.e.*,)—

To use of said Robert Franklyn and his heirs until solemnization of said then intended marriage, and after solemnization thereof,

To use of said Robert Franklyn and his assigns during his life . . . . . remainder,

To use of said Edward Franklyn and Mary Denton during their joint lives and the life of the survivor of them, and after the death of the survivor of them,

To the use of the heirs male of the body of said Edward Franklyn, by said Mary Denton lawfully issuing, and in default or on failure of such issue,

To the use of said Edward Franklyn and the heirs of his body lawfully issuing, and in default of such issue,

To use of Alan Franklyn (the second son of said Robert Franklyn) and the heirs of his body lawfully issuing . . . . . remainder,

To use of said Robert Franklyn, his heirs and assigns, for ever.

Executed by all parties and attested.

Marriage solemnized between said Edward Franklyn and Mary Denton.   1808, July 20th.

Said Robert Franklyn died.   1815, December 5th.

Indentures of lease and release of these dates by the release made between said Edward Franklyn of 1st part, Thomas Hallett, of, &c., of 2nd part, and Peter Clarke, of, &c., of 3rd part.   1817, May 3rd & 4th.

After reciting said abstracted indenture of 19th July, 1808, and reciting that the said Robert Franklyn died on the 8th of December, 1815,

It is witnessed that, for barring all estates in tail of said Edward Franklyn in the hereditaments thereinafter

ABSTRACT No. 6.

described and intended to be thereby granted and conveyed, and all remainders and reversions thereupon expectant or depending, and for limiting said premises, To use of said Edward Franklyn and his heirs, said Edward Franklyn did grant release and confirm unto said Thomas Hallett (in his actual possession then being, &c.) and his heirs,
 All said messuage, lands, and hereditaments before described by a similar description, together, &c., and reversion, &c., and all estate, &c.,
 To hold same unto said Thomas Hallett and his heirs,
 To use of said Thomas Hallett, his heirs and assigns, for ever.

To intent that said Thomas Hallett should become perfect tenant of the freehold of said premises, so that a common recovery with *double voucher* should be suffered of same premises, in which recovery said Peter Clarke should be demandant, said Thomas Hallett tenant, and said Edward Franklyn vouchee, who should vouch the common vouchee.

Declaration that said recovery and all other recoveries, conveyances, fines, and assurances of said premises by or between the parties to abstracting indenture, should operate and enure

Limitation. To use of said Edward Franklyn, his heirs and assigns, for ever.

   Lease executed by said Edward Franklyn, and attested.

   Release executed by all parties, and attested.

The records of the Court of Common Pleas, and of all the other superior Courts, have been carefully searched; but no entry of the proceedings under this recovery deed can be found, nor is any exemplification of the recovery with the deeds.

1818, Said Mary Franklyn (wife of said Edward Franklyn)
November 6th. died.

 There was no issue of said marriage.

1819, By indentures of lease and release of these dates
April 7th & 8th.

ABSTRACT No. 6.   31

respectively made between said Edward Franklyn of one part, and Joseph Bettinson, of   , in the county of   , Esq., of other part,

    Reciting that said Edward Franklyn was seized for an estate of fee simple, in possession of, and in the messuage and hereditaments thereinafter described and intended to be thereby granted and released, and contract to sell same to said Joseph Bettinson for £4,000,

It is by abstracting indenture of release witnessed that in pursuance of said agreement, and in consideration of £4,000 to said Edward Franklyn paid by said Joseph Bettinson, the rect., &c., said Edward Franklyn did grant release and confirm unto said Joseph Bettinson (in his actual possession then being, &c.), and his heirs,

    The said messuage, lands, and premises before described by a similar description.

    [Set out the description].

    Together, &c., and reversion, &c., and all estate, &c.

To hold same premises unto said Joseph Bettinson and his heirs,

To use of said Joseph Bettinson, his heirs and assigns, for ever.

    Covenants by said Edward Franklyn :
      That he was lawfully seized.
      Had power to convey.
      For peaceable possession.
      Freedom from incumbrances.
      And further assurance.

    Lease and release executed by said Edward Franklyn, and attested.

    Receipt endorsed on release for £4,000, signed by Edward Franklyn, and witnessed.

Said Edward Franklyn died without having had any issue.   1820, March 17th. (Evidence.)

He was married only once.

1859.
January 9th.

Probate copy will of said Joseph Bettinson, whereby said testator gave and devised—

> All his messuages, lands, hereditaments, and freehold estates whatsoever

unto his wife Isabella Bettinson during her life; and after her death said testator devised

> All his said freehold and real estates

unto and to the use of Peter Hart and John Thorpe and their heirs for ever,

Upon trust that said Hart and Thorpe, or the survivor of them, or the heirs of such survivor, should, after the death of testator's said wife, Isabella, sell and dispose of his (testator's) freehold estates by public auction or private contract, subject to any conditions, and for such prices as they or he might think proper, and should convey the hereditaments sold to the purchasers thereof.

Declaration that the receipts of said Hart and Thorpe, or survivor of them, or the heirs, executors, or administrators of the survivor, should be a good discharge to purchasers for their purchase monies, and that they should not be bound to see to the application thereof.

Declaration that trustees should stand possessed of the monies to arise from sales, upon trust to pay testator's debts, and funeral and testamentary expenses, and certain legacies in said will mentioned.

And said testator bequeathed his personal estate to his said wife, and appointed her sole executrix of his will.

Signed by said testator, and attested by two witnesses.

1865,
December 14th.

Said Joseph Bettinson died.

1866,
March 24th.

Will of said Joseph Bettinson proved by said Isabella Bettinson in Her Majesty's Court of Probate (Principal Registry.)

1866,
November 19th.

By deed poll of this date, under the hand and seal of the said John Thorpe,

Reciting said abstracted will of said Joseph Bettinson,

And reciting that said Joseph Bettinson died on

the 14th December, 1865, without having revoked or altered his said will,

And reciting that said John Thorpe had never in any respect acted as a trustee of said will, and had wholly refused to act as a trustee of said will,

It was by abstracting deed poll witnessed, that said John Thorpe had from the decease of said Joseph Bettinson absolutely disclaimed and renounced, and did thereby absolutely disclaim and renounce

    All the freehold and real estates whatsoever given or devised by the said recited will of the said Joseph Bettinson, and also the office of trustee of the said will, and all trusts, powers, and authorities whatsoever by the said will expressed to be reposed in or given to the said Peter Hart and John Thorpe, and the survivor of them, and the heirs of such survivor, and all rights and privileges belonging or annexed to the same, or in any wise relating thereto.

Executed by said John Thorpe, and attested.

Said Isabella Bettinson died.   1868, June 9th.

Probate copy will of said Peter Hart, whereby (*inter alia*) said testator devised   1868, November 4th.

    All estates vested in him as a trustee unto Charles Kimber, his heirs and assigns, upon the trusts subsisting thereon at the time of the death of said testator.

Signed by said Peter Hart, and attested by two witnesses.

Said Peter Hart died.   1870, January 9th.

His will proved in Her Majesty's Court of Probate (District Registry of   ).   1873, February 26th.

The estate comprised in the conveyance to Joseph Bettinson by abstracted indentures of 7th and 8th April, 1819, has been contracted to be sold by said Charles Kimber. The question is, whether he can legally exe-

cute the trust for sale contained in the will of Joseph Bettinson, and make a good title to a purchaser, and whether in other respects a good title can be deduced to the estate?
Vide Cooke v. Crawford, 13 Sim. 91; Bradford v. Belfield, 2 Sim. 264; Stevens v. Auston, 30 L. J. (2 B) 212.

No. 7.

FREEHOLD.—Abstract of the Title of Archibald Thomas Denham and his Mortgagee, to a Freehold messuage and land, situate at   , in the parish of D——, in the county of N——.

1826,
November 3rd.

Indenture of feoffment of this date between John Chapman, of   , Esquire, of the one part, and Richard Sandall, of   , Esquire, of other part.

It is witnessed that in consideration of £3,000 to said John Chapman paid by said R. Sandall, at or before, &c., the receipt, &c., said John Chapman did grant, enfeoff, and confirm unto said R. Sandall, his heirs and assigns—

All that messuage or tenement, with the yards, gardens, stables, outbuildings, and appurtenances thereunto adjoining and belonging, and the several closes or fields of land therewith held and enjoyed, containing by estimation sixty acres, situate at   , in the parish of D——, in the county of N——, and then in the occupation of Abraham Reede,

Together, &c., and reversion, &c., and all estate, &c.
To hold same unto and
To the use of said Richard Sandall, his heirs and assigns.

Covenants by said John Chapman:
That he was lawfully seized.
Had power to convey.

ABSTRACT No. 7.

For peaceable possession. Freedom from incumbrances, and further assurance.

   Executed by said John Chapman, and attested.

   Receipt for £3,000 endorsed, signed by said John Chapman, and witnessed.

 Memorandum of livery of seizin, endorsed.

Probate copy will of said Richard Sandall, whereby after bequeathing his personal estate to his wife Jane, subject to payment of his debts and funeral expenses,

 1829, October 23rd.

Said testator gave and devised—
 His messuage, land, and estate, situate at , in the parish of D——, in the county of N——, and all other his freehold and real estate whatsoever, unto his friends Thomas Sims and James Venn, and their heirs,

To the several uses thereinafter declared (that was to say) :—
 To use of said testator's son, Jonathan Sandall, for his life (*sans waste*), and after the determination of that estate by forfeiture or otherwise, in the lifetime of said Jonathan Sandall,
 To use of said Sims and Venn and their heirs during life of said Jonathan Sandall, in trust to preserve the contingent remainders thereinafter limited from being defeated or destroyed . . . remainder,
 To use of the first son of the body of said Jonathan Sandall and the heirs male of the body of such first son lawfully issuing ; and for default of such issue,
 To use of the second, third, fourth, and all and every other the sons and son of the body of said Jonathan Sandall lawfully to be begotten severally and successively, according to seniority of age, and the heirs male of their bodies lawfully issuing; and for default of such issue,
 To the use of all and every the daughter and daughters of the body of said Jonathan Sandall,

 "Purchase."

 "Purchase."

 "Purchase."

lawfully to be begotten, as tenants in common, and of the heirs of their respective bodies lawfully issuing; and, failing issue of any of said daughters,

Then as to the share or shares of such daughter or daughters whose issue should so fail,

"Purchase." To the use of all and every other such daughter or daughters as tenants in common, and of the heirs of their respective bodies lawfully issuing.

And for default of such issue,

"Purchase." To the use of Maria Sandall and Eliza Sandall (said testator's two daughters) to be divided between them, share and share alike, and they to take as tenants in common, and not as joint tenants, and of the several and respective heirs of the bodies of his said daughters lawfully issuing, and, failing issue of either of his said daughters, then, as to the share of such daughter whose issue should so fail,

To the use of the other of his said daughters and the heirs of her body.

And in case both his said daughters should die without issue, then

Limitation in fee in remainder to Christopher.

To the use of testator's brother, Christopher Sandall, his heirs and assigns, for ever.

And said testator appointed said Sims and Venn executors of his will.

Signed and sealed by said testator, and attested by three witnesses.

1853, November 10th Said Richard Sandall died.

1853, December 30th. His said will proved by said Sims and Venn, in the Prerogative Court of the Archbishop of Canterbury.

1838, March 17th. Said Jonathan Sandall (testator's son) intermarried with Mary Potter.

The issue of this marriage were two children only: a son, Frederick Sandall, who was born on the 7th October, 1840, and died on 29th September, 1855 (in the lifetime of his father, Jonathan Sandall).

And a daughter, Caroline Sandall, who was born on 3rd March, 1842, and died on 12th July, 1850, an infant.

Abstract No. 7.

Said Eliza Sandall (one of the testator's daughters) intermarried with Charles Darwin.	1832, May 19th.
The issue of this marriage was one son, Samuel James Darwin, who was born on 23rd April, 1834, and is now living.	
Maria Sandall (the other daughter of the testator, Richard Sandall) intermarried with Benjamin Walton on 3rd January, 1836.	1836, January 3rd.
The only issue of this marriage was a daughter, Frances Walton, who was born on 20th June, 1837.	
Said Frances Walton died without issue, and unmarried.	1858, July 19th.
Said Maria Walton died, leaving her daughter surviving.	1856, August 4th.
Said Jonathan Sandall died without leaving any issue surviving.	1860, August 17th.
Said Eliza Darwin died, leaving her husband, Charles Darwin, and her only child, Samuel James Darwin, her surviving, who are both now living.	1862, February 22nd
By indenture of this date, made between said Samuel James Darwin of the one part, and Thomas Ross, of, &c., of other part—	1863, November 9th.

It is witnessed that for the purpose of destroying and defeating all estates in tail, of or to which said Samuel James Darwin was entitled in the hereditaments thereinafter described, and all estates, rights, interests, and powers, to take effect after the determination or in defeasance of such estates tail, and for assuring and limiting the inheritance in fee simple, in possession of and in the said hereditaments, to the use and in manner thereinafter expressed, and in consideration of 10s. to said Samuel James Darwin paid by said Thomas Ross (the receipt, &c.), said Samuel James Darwin did grant release and confirm to said Thomas Ross and his heirs—

> All said messuage and lands comprised in said abstracted indenture of feoffment of 3rd November, 1826, by a similar description,
> Which said messuage, land, and premises were formerly in occupation of Abraham Reid, since of said Richard Sandall, and then of said Samuel

PEDIGREE OF SANDALL FAMILY.

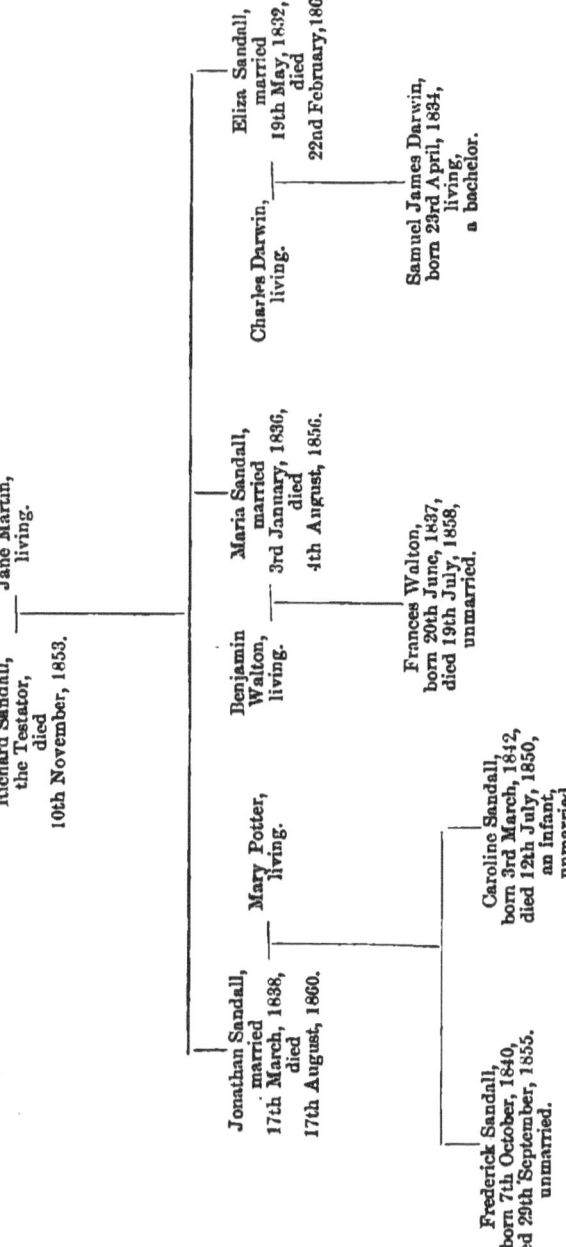

ABSTRACT No. 7. 39

James Darwin. [Set out full description of parcels.]

Together, &c., and the reversion, &c., and all estate, &c.

To hold same unto said Thomas Ross and his heirs (freed and discharged from all estates in tail of said Samuel James Darwin, and all other estates, rights, interests, and powers, to take effect upon the determination, or in defeasance of such estates tail),

To the use of said Samuel James Darwin, his heirs and assigns, for ever.

Declaration by said Samuel James Darwin (who was then a bachelor), that no widow of his should be entitled to dower out of said hereditaments, or any part thereof.

Executed by said Samuel James Darwin, and attested.

Enrolled in Chancery pursuant to 3rd and 4th W. 4, c. 74, 14th March, 1864.

1864;
March 14th.

By indenture of this date, made between said Samuel James Darwin, of one part, and Archibald Thomas Denham, of, &c., of other part,

1864,
May 29th.

Reciting that said Samuel James Darwin was seized of the messuage, lands, and hereditaments thereinafter described, and intended to be thereby conveyed for an estate of inheritance in fee simple, in possession, free from all incumbrances,

And reciting that at a sale by auction of said premises on the 4th October then last, said Archibald Thomas Denham was the highest bidder for and declared to be one purchaser of said messuage, lands, and premises, with the appurtenances, at the price of £5,000,

It is by abstracting indenture witnessed, that in consideration of £5,000 to said Samuel James Darwin paid by said Thomas Denham, at or before, &c. (the receipt, &c.) said Samuel James Darwin did grant, convey, and confirm unto said Archibald Thomas Denham and his heirs,

All said messuage, lands, and hereditaments before described by a similar description.

Together, &c., and all estate, &c.

To hold same premises to said Archibald Thomas Denham and his heirs,

    To such uses, upon and for such trusts, intents, and purposes, and with under and subject to such powers, provisoes, declarations, and agreements, as said Archibald Thomas Denham should by any deed or deeds, with or without power of revocation and new appointment, to be by him duly executed from time to time, direct or appoint, and for default of and until such direction or appointment, and so far as no such direction or appointment should extend,

"Limitation."   To the use of said Archibald Thomas Denham, his heirs and assigns, for ever.

Covenants by said Samuel James Darwin :
That he had power to grant and convey.
For peaceable possession.
Freedom from incumbrances.
And for further assurance.

    Executed by both parties, and attested.

    Receipt for £5,000 endorsed, signed by said Samuel James Darwin, and witnessed.

1870,
March 23rd.

By indenture of mortgage of this date, made between said Archibald Thomas Denham, of one part, and Arthur Lorton, of, &c., of other part,

It is witnessed that in consideration of £2,000 to said Archibald Thomas Denham paid by said Arthur Lorton, the receipt, &c., said Archibald Thomas Denham did direct and appoint, and also grant and convey to said Arthur Lorton and his heirs,

    All said messuage, lands, and premises hereinbefore described by a similar description, together, &c., and all estate, &c.

To hold same unto and to the use of said Arthur Lorton, his heirs and assigns, for ever,

    Subject to a proviso in indenture now in recital contained for redemption of said premises on payment by said Archibald Thomas Denham, his heirs, executors, administrators, or assigns, to said Arthur Lorton, his executors, administrators, or assigns, of £2,000, on 23rd September, 1870, with interest at 5 per cent.

Usual mortgage covenants.

Power of sale.

> Executed by said Archibald Thomas Denham, and attested.

> Receipt for £2,000 endorsed, signed by said A. Thomas Denham, and witnessed.

Mr. Archibald Thomas Denham has contracted to sell the property to Mr. A—— B—— for £6,000, the mortgage debt of £2,000 and interest to be paid off out of purchase-money.

No. 8.

FREEHOLD TITLE.—Abstract of the Title of the Heir-at-Law of Mr. Samuel Adams to a Freehold farm and estate, called Mason's Farm, situate in the parish of R——, in the county of L——.

1818, June 1st. Conveyance by Fine and Declaration of uses.

By indenture of this date, made between Joseph Mason, of   , in the county of   , Esq., and Julia his wife, of one part, and Samuel Adams, of   , in the county of   , Gentleman, of other part,

> Reciting that under the will of her father, Jacob Smith, deceased, bearing date the 14th November, 1806, said Julia Mason was seized in fee simple in possession of the messuage, farm, and hereditaments thereinafter described,

> And reciting contract for sale of said premises to said Samuel Adams for £7,000,

It is by abstracting indenture witnessed that in pursuance of said agreement, and in consideration of £7,000 of lawful money, &c., paid by said Samuel Adams to said Joseph Mason and Julia his wife, at or before, &c., the receipt, &c., said Joseph Mason, with privity and approbation of said Julia his wife (she thereby consenting thereto), did covenant with said Samuel Adams, and his heirs and assigns, that said Joseph Mason and Julia his wife, or her heirs, would, at the costs of said Joseph Mason, as of Easter term then last, or in or as of the then present Trinity term, or of some other subsequent term, acknowledge and levy before His Majesty's Justices of the Court of Common Pleas at Westminster unto said Samuel Adams and his heirs one or more fine or fines sur conuzance de droit come ceo, &c., whereupon proclamations should be had, &c., of and concerning—

> All that messuage, out-buildings, and estate, and the several closes, inclosures, lands and grounds held, occupied, and enjoyed therewith, commonly called or known by the name of Mason's Farm, situate, lying, and being in the township of   , in the parish of R——, in the county of L——, and which several lands and grounds were called or known by the several names of, &c. [set out names of fields, &c.], and contained altogether by estimation 450 acres, and were formerly in the tenure or occupation of the said Jacob Smith and then of the said Samuel Adams.

Together with all houses, &c.

Declaration that said fine and all other fines, conveyances, and assurances of said hereditaments and premises should operate and enure

> To the use of said Samuel Adams, his heirs and assigns for ever.

Covenants by said Joseph Mason with said Samuel Adams, his heirs and assigns:

That said Joseph Mason and Julia his wife, in her right, were lawfully seized.

That he and his wife had power to convey.

For peaceable possession.

Free from incumbrances.

And for further assurance.

> Executed by said Joseph Mason and Julia Mason, and attested.
>
> Receipt for £7,000 indorsed. Signed by Joseph Mason and Julia Mason, and witnessed.

ABSTRACT No. 8.

Trinity Term,
58th George 3rd.

Chirograph indentures of fine, wherein said Samuel Adams is Plaintiff and said Joseph Mason and Julia his wife are Deforceants. Of—
Two messuages, two barns, two stables, two cowhouses, 500 acres of land, 100 acres of meadow, 100 acres of pasture, common of pasture and turbary, in the parish of R——, in the county of L——.

Delivered with proclamations.

Probate copy will of said Samuel Adams, whereby, after bequeathing his personal estate to his father, Noah Adams, and appointing him sole executor,
Said testator devised—
All that his messuage, farm, and freehold estate, called Mason's Farm, situate in the parish of R——, in the county of L——, and all other his real estates,
Unto his mother, Sarah Adams, during her natural life for her sole use.
(N.B.—The will contains no further devise of real estates.)

1826,
November 4th.

Signed by said Samuel Adams,
and attested by three witnesses.

Said Samuel Adams died a bachelor.

1830,
November 23rd.

Said will proved by said Noah Adams in Consistory Court of Bishop of L——.

1830,
December 17th.

Said Sarah Adams died.

1868,
February 4th.

Probate copy will of Titus Adams, of   , in the county of   .

1848,
January 17th.

Whereby testator gave and devised
All his messuages, lands, and real estates whatsoever and wheresoever, and all his personal estate,
Unto his daughter, Rebecca Adams, her heirs, executors, administrators, and assigns.
And he appointed his said daughter sole executrix of his will.

Signed by said Titus Adams,
and attested by two witnesses.

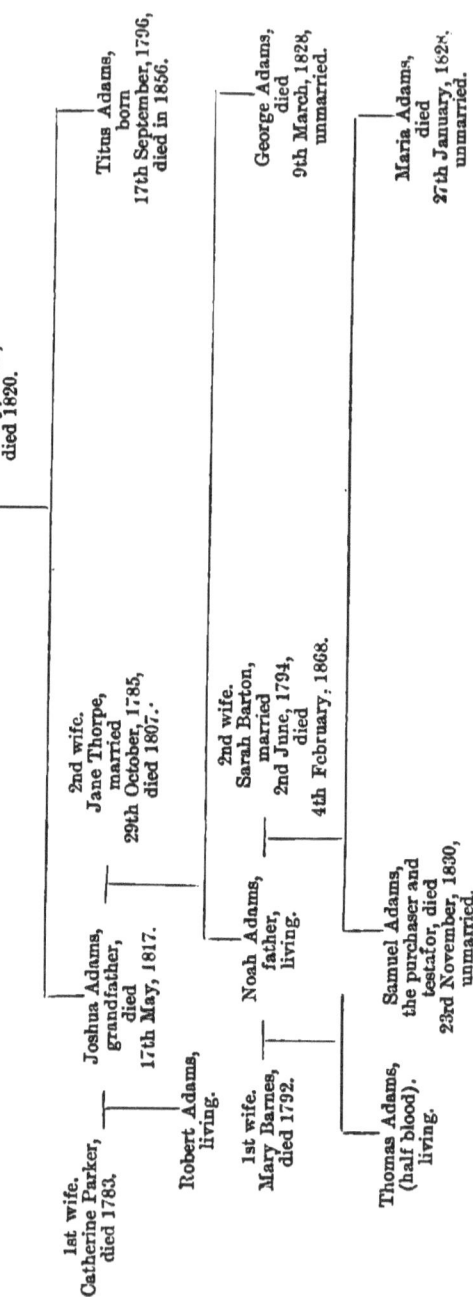

Said Titus Adams died.

1856,
December 20th

Said will proved by said Rebecca Adams in Consistory Court of Bishop of   .

1857,
February 8th.

See pedigree of Adams family.

Samuel Adams, the purchaser in 1818 and the testator of 1826, died in 1830, intestate as to the remainder in fee in the estate after the death of his mother, Sarah Adams.

It is now requisite to ascertain who was the heir-at-law of Samuel Adams at the time of his death, and to whom the estate now belongs.

From the pedigree it appears that Noah Adams (the father of Samuel Adams) and Thomas Adams (the brother of the half blood of Samuel Adams) are both living.

Read the canons or rules of descent, as stated by Sir William Blackstone.

No. 9.

COPYHOLD TITLE.—Abstract of the Title of Mr. Thomas Denton and Mrs. Joanna Denton to a Copyhold or customary messuage and farm called Mertons, situate in the manor and parish of T——, in the county of N——.

Manor of T——,
county of N——.

At a General Court then held for said manor, the homage presented that on the 4th day of August then last Thomas Thorpe and Martha his wife (she, the said Martha, being first solely and secretly examined by the steward of said manor, apart from her said husband, and thereby concealing) did surrender into the hands of the lord of the manor by the rod, by the hands and acceptance of said steward, according to the custom of said manor,

1810,
November 7th.

All that customary tenement and 90 acres of land

customary and heriotable, called Mertons, with the appurtenances, situate and being in the said manor and lying near the windmill there, and bounded on the north and west by the river S——,

Together, &c., and the reversion, &c., and all estate, &c.,

To the use of Charles Denton, of   , gentleman, his heirs and assigns, for ever; whereupon came said Charles Denton and humbly prayed to be admitted tenant to said premises.

To whom the lord granted seizin thereof by the rod. To hold same, with the appurtenances, unto said Charles Denton, his heirs and assigns, for ever, by the rod, at the will of the lord according to the custom of said manor, &c., and he gave to the lord of said manor for a fine as appears in margin, and so was thereof admitted tenant.

And his fealty was respited.

Same Court.   Said Charles Denton surrendered—
All his messuages, lands, and tenements holden of said manor,
To the use of his will.

1830,   Probate copy will of said Charles Denton of this date.
May 4th.   Whereby testator devised and gave
All his freehold and copyhold and real and personal estate whatsoever,
Unto his wife Sarah Denton during her life, and after her death,
Unto testator's second son Jeremiah Denton, his heirs and assigns, for ever.

Signed by said Charles Denton, and attested by one witness only.

1832,   Said Charles Denton died.
October 17th.

1832,   Said will proved by Sarah Denton (the executrix
December 3rd.   therein named), in the Consistory Court of the Bishop of L——.

1833,   At a General Court then held for said manor, after
February 27th.   presenting the death of said Charles Denton seized of (amongst other hereditaments),
Said messuage and land called Mertons, before

described, to which said Charles Denton was admitted at a court held on 7th November, 1810,

And also presenting and setting out said will of said Charles Denton,

The said Sarah Denton prayed the lord to be admitted tenant

> To said messuage and lands called Mertons, whereof said Charles Denton died seized.

To whom the lord by his steward granted seizin thereof by the rod,

To hold same unto said Sarah Denton during her life; and after her death to said Jeremiah Denton, his heirs and assigns, for ever, according to custom of said manor, subject to the yearly rent of 20s., fealty suit of court, &c.

And she gave to the lord for a fine, &c., and was admitted tenant accordingly.

Said Sarah Denton died.   1840, August 9th.

By conditional surrender of this date said Jeremiah Denton, in consideration of £1,000 to him paid by Richard Marton, of, &c., did out of court surrender into the hands of the lord of said manor by the rod, according to custom of said manor,   1845. March 25th.

> All before-described copyhold messuage and lands, called Mertons.
>
> Together, &c., and reversion, &c., and all estate, &c.

To the use of said Richard Marton, his heirs and assigns, for ever.

> Proviso for making said surrender void on payment by said Jeremiah Denton, his heirs, executors, administrators, or assigns, to said Richard Marton, his executors, administrators, or assigns, of £1,000, with interest after the rate of £5 per centum per annum, on 25th September then next.
>
> Signed by said Jeremiah Denton.
>
> Receipt for £1,000 endorsed, signed, and witnessed.

Enrolled on court roll of said manor on 3rd September, 1845.

48 ABSTRACT No. 9.

1856,
May 3rd.

Probate copy will of said Jeremiah Denton of this date.

Testator charged his messuage or tenement and lands, called Mertons, copyhold held of manor of T——, and all other his real estates, with the payment to his daughter Maria Denton of an annuity of £200 during her life, with powers of distress and entry for recovery of same annuity.

Subject to said annuity, said testator gave and devised all his said copyhold and real estates to his two sons Thomas Denton and Robert Denton, their heirs and assigns, for ever, in equal shares as tenants in common, subject to said mortgage to said Richard Marton for securing £1,000 and interest.

And said testator appointed his said two sons executors of his said will.

Signed by said Jeremiah Denton,
and attested by two witnesses.

Manor of T——,
county of N——.

1857,
August 17th.

By an authority in writing, said Richard Marton acknowledged to have received from said Jeremiah Denton the sum of £1,000 and interest due thereon, secured to be paid to said Richard Marton by virtue of a certain conditional surrender dated the 25th of March, 1845, made by said Jeremiah Denton (and enrolled on court rolls of the said manor on 3rd September, 1845) of the messuage and lands called Mertons, comprised in such conditional surrender. And said Richard Marton thereby authorised and empowered the steward of the court of said manor for the time being to enter satisfaction on the court rolls of said manor for payment of said sum of £1,000 and all interest due and owing in respect thereof, by virtue of said conditional surrender.

Signed by said Richard Marton.

1860,
April 23rd.

Probate copy will of said Robert Denton,

Whereby testator gave and devised to his wife Joanna Denton the whole of his estate and effects of whatsoever description which he might be possessed of or entitled to at the time of his decease.

And the testator thereby appointed Arthur Denton, his cousin, sole executor of his said will.

Signed by said Robert Denton,
and attested by two witnesses.

Said Robert Denton died (in the life-time of his father, said Jeremiah Denton), leaving his wife, said Joanna Denton, and four children, him surviving.   1860, November 4th.

Letters of administration of the personal estate of said Robert Denton (with will annexed) granted to said Joanna Denton by Her Majesty's Court of Probate (District Registry of   ), said Arthur Denton, the executor named in said will, having died in testator's life-time.   1861, January 28th

Said Jeremiah Denton died.   1866, February 2nd.

Said will of said Jeremiah Denton proved by said Thomas Denton in Court of Probate (District Registry of   ).   1866, April 14th.

Manor of P———,
county of N———.

At a General Court then held for said manor,   1866, September 28th

   Reciting that at a court held on 27th February, 1833, Sarah Denton, as the devisee for life named in the will of her husband Charles Denton, was admitted tenant for her life, with remainder to the use of her son Jeremiah Denton, his heirs and assigns, to

   All that customary tenement and 90 acres of land called Mertons, &c. [same description as in abstracted admission of 7th November, 1810],

And presenting death of said Sarah Denton on 9th August, 1840,

And also presenting and setting out said abstracted will of Jeremiah Denton and his death,

And also presenting and setting out said abstracted will of said Robert Denton and his death,

It was set out that on 26th September, 1866, said Thomas Denton and Joanna Denton came before A. B., gentleman, deputy-steward of the courts of this manor, and pursuant to the provisions contained in an act of parliament passed in the 4th and 5th years of the reign of her present Majesty Queen Victoria, humbly prayed to be admitted tenants to

All that the said copyhold tenement and 90 acres of land called Mertons, &c., to which said Jeremiah Denton was admitted tenant as aforesaid, and which was so devised to said Thomas Denton and Robert Denton by said abstracted will of said Jeremiah Denton, deceased, as aforesaid.

To which said Thomas Denton and Joanna Denton the lord of said manor, by his said deputy-steward, did by virtue of said act out of court grant and deliver seizin of said premises by the rod,

To hold said customary tenement and premises, with the appurtenances, unto said Thomas Denton and Joanna Denton, their heirs and assigns, as tenants in common (subject as in said will of said Jeremiah Denton is mentioned) of the lord, according to the custom of said manor, by copy of court roll, &c.; and they gave to the lord for a fine for such their estate and entry on premises as appears in the margin. And said Thomas Denton and Joanna Denton were admitted tenants of the premises aforesaid, in form aforesaid, &c.

1871,
April 23rd.
Said Maria Denton, the annuitant, died.

No. 10.

PERSONALTY.—REVERSIONARY INTEREST IN CONSOLS.—Abstract of the Title of Mr. Edwin Dermer to the reversion of and in a moiety of £4,850 Three per Cent. Consolidated Annuities, standing in the names of the Reverend Francis Ashworth and Alfred Clift, Esquire, as trustees of the will of Martin Oliver, Esquire, deceased.

1858,
June 9th.
Martin Oliver, of   , in the county of   , Esquire, made his will of this date, and thereby (*inter alia*) directed his executors to

set apart and appropriate out of his estate the sum of £5,000 Three per Cent. Consolidated Annuities, in the names of the Reverend Francis Ashworth and Alfred Clift, Esquire, which sum of £5,000 stock the testator declared should be held by them upon trust, to pay the dividends and income thereof to his, the testator's, sister Sarah Sanby, during her life, for her separate use, without power of anticipation; and after her death the said sum of £5,000 Consols to be held by the said trustees upon trust for the said testator's nephew, Charles Sanby, and testator's niece, Fanny Louisa Dermer, the wife of Edwin Dermer, in equal shares, as tenants in common. And the said testator appointed the Reverend Francis Ashworth and Alfred Clift executors of his said will.

Signed by said testator,
and witnessed by two witnesses.

Said Martin Oliver died.   1858, November 17th

Said will proved in Her Majesty's Court of Probate, at Principal Registry, by said executors.   1858, December 20th.

By indenture of this date, made between said Edwin Dermer, of   , of   , of first part, said Fanny Louisa Dermer (wife of said Edwin Dermer), of second part, Richard Dryden, of, &c., third part, and Thomas Terry, of, &c., fourth part,   1868, March 4th.

Reciting said abstracted will of said Martin Oliver, and his death and proof of his will,

And reciting that the legacy duties, payable to Government in respect of the said sum of £5,000 Consols bequeathed by the said will, required the sale of £150 Consols to provide for the payment thereof and of the legal expenses incidental thereto, and that accordingly the sum of £150 Consols (part of such sum of £5,000 Consols) had been sold out by the executors of the will of the said Martin Oliver, and the produce thereof had been applied by such executors in payment of such legacy duties and expenses; and that the sum of £4,850 Consols (being the residue of such sum of £5,000 Consols, after the raising and payment of such legacy duties and expenses) had been transferred by the said executors into and was then standing in the joint names of the said Francis Ashworth and Alfred Clift, upon the trusts declared by the said will, concerning the said sum of £5,000 Consols and the dividends and income thereof, and reciting that, under the trusts of the said will, the said Fanny Louisa Dermer was entitled to the sum of £2,425 Consols, being one moiety of the said sum of £4,850 Consols (subject to the life interest therein of said Sarah Sanby). And that, in case the said Edwin Dermer should survive the said Sarah Sanby, he would, in right of his said wife, become absolutely entitled in possession to such sum of £2,425 Consols, subject to the equity of his said wife to a settlement thereout on herself and her children,

And reciting that said Edwin Dermer and Fanny Louisa, his wife, were desirous of settling and assuring (*inter alia*) their said respective reversionary interests in · (*inter alia*) said sum of £2,425 Consols, or other the trust fund for the time being representing the same in manner thereinafter expressed, and that they had agreed that such sum of £2,425 Consols should be assigned to and vested in a trustee, in trust for the said Edwin Dermer, for his absolute benefit;

It was by abstracting indenture witnessed that, for the purpose of partly effectuating the said desire, and in consideration of the premises, and in pursuance and exercise of the power or authority in this behalf given to or vested in the said Fanny Louisa Dermer by the Act of Parliament 21st Victoria cap. 57,* and of every other power or authority enabling her in that behalf, she, the said Fanny Louisa Dermer, with the concurrence of said Edwin Dermer (testified by his execution thereof), did thereby assign and dispose of, and said Edwin Dermer did thereby assign and confirm unto said Richard Dryden, his executors, administrators, and assigns—

* 21st Vic. cap. 57. This act enables *femmes couvertes* to assign certain reversionary interests in personalty, by a deed acknowledged with such formalities as are provided in the Fines and Recoveries Act (Act B). But see the exceptions in the last section of the Act.

ABSTRACT No. 10.

All that the said sum of £2,425 Three per Cent. Consolidated Bank Annuities, being the one moiety or equal half-part of the said Fanny Louisa Dermer and of the said Edwin Dermer, in her right of and in the said sum of £4,850 Consols (or other the trust fund for the time being representing the same) then standing in the names of the said Francis Ashworth and Alfred Clift upon the trusts in and by said will of said Martin Oliver declared of said sum of £5,000 Consols as aforesaid, and the dividends and annual income thereof, and all the right and interest of said Edwin Dermer and Fanny Louisa, his wife, and each of them, to and in said sum of £2,425 Consols and dividends hereby assigned;

To hold and take said sum of £2,425 Consols, or other fund for the time being representing the same, and the dividends thereof thereinbefore assigned (subject to the life interest of said Sarah Sanby therein) unto said Richard Dryden, his executors, administrators, and assigns,

 In trust for said Edwin Dermer, his executors, administrators, and assigns, for his and their absolute benefit, and to be assigned and disposed of as he or they should direct.

N.B.—This settlement also contained certain provisions for Mrs. Dermer and her children from other property.

     Executed by all parties, and attested.

Acknowledged by said Fanny Louisa Dermer, pursuant to provisions of said Act of 21 Vict. c. 57.

This deed, marked A, was this day produced before us and acknowledged by Fanny Louisa Dermer, the wife of Edwin Dermer, therein named, to be her act and deed, previous to which acknowledgment the said Fanny Louisa Dermer was examined by us separately and apart from her said husband, touching her knowledge of the contents of the said deed and her consent thereto, and declared the same to be freely and voluntarily executed by her.

Certificate endorsed.

Witness our hands this 4th day of March, 1868.

    A—— B——
    C—— D—— } Commissioners, &c.

No. 11.

LEASEHOLD FOR YEARS.—Abstract of the Title of Mr. Clement Morgan to two Leasehold messuages, situate in Lorton Road, in the parish of   , in the county of Surrey (being Nos. 8 and 9 in Lorton Road).

1856,
June 24th.

By indenture of lease of this date made between Adam Adams, of, &c., Esq., of one part, and Robert Thornton, of, &c., builder, of other part,

It is witnessed that in consideration of the expense the said Robert Thornton had incurred in erecting and finishing the two messuages thereinafter devised, and also in consideration of the rent and covenants thereinafter reserved and contained, said A. Adams did grant and demise to said Robert Thornton,

All that piece or parcel of ground situate and being in Lorton Road, in the parish of   , in the county of Surrey, measuring in the front next the said road 150 feet of assize, and in depth from north to south 300 feet (more or less), and the two messuages or tenements then standing and being on said piece of ground, and known as Nos. 8 and 9 in Lorton Road aforesaid, with the appurtenances,

To hold said premises to said Robert Thornton, his executors, administrators, and assigns for 99 years, to be computed from the 24th day of June, 1855,

Yielding and paying to said A. Adams, his heirs and assigns, the yearly rent of £30, payable quarterly.

Covenants by said lessee :
To pay rent and taxes.
To repair and paint.
To insure in £500 in joint names of lessor and lessee.
To surrender at end of term.
Proviso for re-entry for non-payment of rent, &c.
Covenant by lessor for quiet enjoyment.

Executed by said lessor and attested.

1864,
November 14th

Probate copy will of said Robert Thornton.
Whereby (*inter alia*) he gave and bequeathed his two leasehold messuages and ground, being Nos. 8 and 9

Abstract No. 11.

in Lorton Road, in the county of Surrey, unto his executors thereinafter named, for all his estate, term, and interest thereon at the time of his decease, upon trust, to pay the net rents and profits thereof (after payment of ground-rent, insurance, and repairs) unto testator's daughter, Mary Robinson, during her life, for her sole and separate use; and after her decease the said leasehold messuages were to be held in trust for the children of testator's daughter, Mary Robinson, in equal shares, and testator appointed Robert Pember, of, &c., and Charles Norris, of, &c., executors of his said will.

Said Robert Thornton died. 1865, February 4th.

By indenture of this date made between the said Robert Pember, of one part, and Jonathan Latham, of, &c., of other part, 1865, April 17th.

 Reciting said abstracted indenture of lease, and said will of said Robert Thornton, and reciting contract for sale of said leasehold messuages by said Robert Pember to said Jonathan Latham for £800,

It is by abstracting indenture witnessed that in consideration of £800 paid by said Jonathan Latham to said Robert Pember (as such executor as aforesaid), the receipt, &c., said Robert Pember (as such executor of will of said Robert Thornton) did grant and assign to said Jonathan Latham

 All that the said piece of ground and the two messuages thereon, Nos. 8 and 9 in Lorton Road, in the parish of   , in the county of Surrey, and all other the premises comprised in and demised by the said recited indenture of lease, together with the lessee's fixtures and appurtenances, and all estate, &c., of said Robert Pember (as such executor as aforesaid) in said premises,

To hold same unto said Jonathan Latham, his executors, administrators, and assigns, for all residue of said term of 99 years, subject to payment of said rent of £30 and performance of lessee's covenants.

Covenant by said Robert Pember that he had not encumbered.

ABSTRACT No. 11.

Covenant by Jonathan Latham for payment of rent and performance of covenants.

Executed by Robert Pember and Jonathan Latham, and attested.

Receipt for £800 endorsed, signed by said Robert Pember, and witnessed.

1866,
November 9th. Said Charles Norris renounced probate of said will.

1867,
January 29th. Said Robert Pember died without having proved said will.

1867,
June 3rd. Letters of administration of the personal estate of said Robert Thornton (with the said will annexed) were granted to Catherine Thornton, the widow and relict of said Robert Thornton, by Her Majesty's Court of Probate at the Principal Registry.

1868,
May 4th. By indenture of this date made between said Jonathan Latham (therein called the mortgagor) of the first part, and A——, of   , B——, of   , and C——, of   , trustees of the   Permanent Mutual Benefit Building Society (thereinafter called the mortgagees), of the second part,

After reciting said abstracted lease,

And reciting said recited will of said Robert Thornton,

And reciting said abstracted indenture of 17th April, 1865,

And reciting that the mortgagor, as the owner of ten shares in the said society, numbered respectively   , was by virtue of the rules of the said society entitled to receive out of the funds thereof the sum of £500 on account of the said ten shares, subject to the payments and subscriptions at the rate class   , mentioned in the said rules, for the term of   years from the   day of   , 186 , to be secured in manner thereinafter mentioned.

It is by abstracting indenture witnessed that in consideration of the sum of £500 sterling to the mortgagor paid by mortgagees as such trustees as aforesaid, the receipt, &c., the said mortgagor did grant and demise unto the mortgagees, their executors, administrators, and assigns,

All that the said piece or parcel of ground thereinbefore described and comprised in and demised by the said thereinbefore recited indenture of lease of the 24th day of June, 1856; and the two messuages or tenements then erected and standing thereon, and known as Nos. 8 and 9, in Lorton Road aforesaid, with the fixtures, rights, easements, and appurtenances thereto belonging,

To hold the same leasehold premises unto the said mortgagees, their executors, administrators, and assigns thenceforth during all the unexpired residue of the said term of 99 years, by the said lease granted (save and except the last ten days of said term).

And to hold the said fixtures absolutely, subject as to the same leasehold premises and fixtures to the powers, provisoes, and agreements thereinafter contained.

Proviso and agreement that if the mortgagor, his executors, administrators, or assigns, should duly make and pay the several subscriptions, fines, and other payments, and observe and comply with the regulations prescribed, or to be prescribed, in the rules of the said society, in respect of said ten shares, and should perform the covenants on his part thereinafter contained, then the mortgagees, or the persons representing them, should at the costs of the mortgagee, his executors, administrators, or assigns, revest the said premises and fixtures in the mortgagor, his executors, administrators, and assigns.

Proviso for quiet enjoyment by said mortgagor, his executors, administrators, or assigns, on payment of said subscriptions and compliance with said regulations.

Proviso that in case the mortgagor, his executors, administrators, or assigns, should fail, neglect, or refuse for the space of three calendar months to make and pay all or any of the subscriptions, fines, or other payments which should become due to said society in respect of said ten shares, or should fail to comply with any of the said regulations, or to perform and observe any of his covenants thereinafter contained, or should fail, neglect, or refuse to perform, fulfil, and keep all and every the covenants, conditions, provisoes, and agreements in recited lease contained, and on his part as assignee to be performed, then, and in any or either of

said cases it should be lawful for the mortgagees, or
the trustees or trustee for the time being of said society,
at any time or times thereafter, when and as they or
he should (*inter alia*) in their discretion think fit, and
without the consent of said mortgagor, his executors,
or administrators, to sell and absolutely dispose of said
leasehold premises, or any part thereof, for all the
residue then unexpired therein of the term thereby
created, and the said fixtures absolutely, either altogether
or in lots, at one or at separate times, by public auction
or by private contract, or partly by each of those modes,
for the most money that could be reasonably gotten for
the same, and subject or not subject to any special conditions
relative to the title or otherwise, with liberty to
buy in, &c., and to assign and assure said leasehold messuages
and premises when sold to the purchaser or purchasers
thereof for all the residue of the said term by
abstracting indenture granted.

Proviso and agreement that abstracting indenture
should be read and construed in all respects as if the
following rules of said society, viz., the whole of the
rules Nos. 30, 31, and 32, had been incorporated therein
and made in terms specially applicable to said premises
and to the security thereby made. (By rule , every
receipt of the trustee or trustees for the time being shall
be good and sufficient discharge to the purchaser paying
his purchase-money, who shall not be obliged to see to
the application of the same, nor be required to see
whether any or what money shall be due under such
mortgage, whether there has or has not been any breach
on the part of any such mortgagor of the rules of the
society, or of the provisions of such mortgage deed, but
the possession of the title deeds and mortgage deeds,
and the written instructions of the board, shall be considered
sufficient authority for disposing of the premises
by the trustees.

Mortgage covenants.

Power of Attorney as to reversion of 10 days.

And inasmuch as a period of ten days was excepted
from the grant and demise thereby made, and it was
thereby further agreed that said mortgagor should stand
possessed of such ten days upon trust for the purposes
of abstracting security and be assigned and disposed of
accordingly, and that all and every the powers therein-

ABSTRACT No. 11. 59

before given for the purposes of such security should
override and comprise such ten days in the same manner in all respects as if the same had formed part of said
mortgaged premises; and for the purpose of facilitating
the execution of such powers and every or any of them,
the mortgagor did thereby nominate and appoint the
mortgagees, their executors, administrators, and assigns,
or any or either of them, or the trustees for the time
being of the said society, to be the attorneys or attorney
of him, the mortgagor, his executors, administrators,
and assigns, in his or their name or names, and as his
and their act and deed, to assign and assure, as such
attorneys or attorney should think fit, the said reversionary estate, or interest of ten days excepted and
reserved out of the grant and demise thereby made or
expressed, and intended so to be, and to sign, seal, and
deliver any deed or other instrument for that purpose.

Executed by said Jonathan Latham,
and attested.

Said C ——(one of the trustees of said society) died. 1870,
March 14th.

D——, of, &c., was duly appointed a trustee of said 1870,
society, in the place or stead of said C——. March 30th.

By indenture of this day made between said A——, 1871,
B——, and D—— (therein described as trustees of the June 19th.
said   Permanent Mutual Benefit Building Society),
of first part, said Jonathan Latham of second part, and
Clement Morgan, of, &c., of third part,

After reciting said abstracted lease of 24th June,
1856, and said will and assignment to Jonathan
Latham, and reciting said indenture of mortgage
of 4th May, 1868, and reciting that said C——
died on the 14th day of March, 1870, and that
said D—— was on 30th day of same month duly
appointed a trustee of said society, and reciting
that default having been made by said Jonathan
Latham for more than   calendar months in
payment and observance of the subscriptions,
fines, and regulations of said society, and on his
part to be paid and observed, and the rent of
the said leasehold premises being insufficient, the
said parties to abstracting indenture of first part
(as such trustees as aforesaid) had (in exercise of

the said power of sale, and pursuant to the written instructions or resolution of the board of directors of said society) agreed with said Clement Morgan for the absolute sale to him of the said leasehold messuages and premises comprised in the said recited indenture of lease of the 24th day of June, 1856, for the residue of the said term of 99 years, created by the same indenture of lease, at the price of £700, and that the said Jonathan Latham had agreed to concur therein for the purpose of assigning the said reversionary term of ten days in the said leasehold premises, and to the intent that the whole residue of said term of 99 years should be vested in the said Clement Morgan;

It is by abstracting indenture witnessed that in consideration of £700 by said Clement Morgan that day paid to said parties thereto of first part (as such trustees of said society as aforesaid), the receipt, &c., the said A——, B——, and D—— (as to the term and interest vested in them) did thereby assign, and said Jonathan Latham (as to said reversionary term of ten days, and as to all other the premises and terms then vested in him) did assign and confirm, and the said Jonathan Latham (by the said A——, as his attorney, so far as related to said reversionary term of ten days in the said leasehold messuages and premises comprised in said mortgage) did assign to said Clement Morgan

All that the said piece of ground and two messuages or tenements known as Nos. 8 and 9 in Lorton Road aforesaid, and all other the leasehold premises comprised in the said recited indenture of lease of the 24th day of June, 1856, with the fixtures and appurtenances in and to said premises belonging,

And all estate, term of years, &c.

To hold the said leasehold and other premises thereby assigned unto said Clement Morgan, his executors, administrators, and assigns, during all residue then to come and unexpired of said term of 99 years, created by the said recited indenture of lease of 24th day of June, 1856 (freed and discharged from said recited indenture of mortgage and mortgage debt, thereby secured, and all interest, claims, and demands in respect thereof), subject to the payment (as from the 24th day of June then next) of the rent, and to the performance of the lessee's covenants reserved and contained by and in said recited indenture of lease.

Covenants by A——, B——, and D——, that they had not encumbered.

Covenants for title (leasehold) by said Jonathan Latham.

Covenant by Clement Morgan to pay rent and perform covenants in lease.

> Executed by said A——, B——, and D——, and by said Jonathan Latham and Clement Morgan, and by said Jonathan Latham by said A——, as his attorney, and attested.

> Receipt endorsed for £700, signed by said A——, B——, and D——, and witnessed.

No. 12.

POLICY OF LIFE ASSURANCE.—Abstract of Title to a Policy of Assurance for £2,000 in   Life Assurance Company on life of Reverend Tobias Wrayson.

By a policy of assurance, No. 1,460, under the hands and seals of three of the directors of the   Life Assurance Company, whereby

1850, May 17th.

The funds and property of the said company were, in consideration of the annual premium of £   , made subject and liable to the payment to the executors, administrators, or assigns of the Reverend Tobias Wrayson, Hastings, in the county of Sussex, clerk, within three calendar months after satisfactory proof should have been received at the office of said company of decease of said Tobias Wrayson, of the sum of £2,000 and such further sum or sums as should under the regulations of said company be appropriated as a bonus to said policy.

> Executed by three directors of said company.

ABSTRACT No. 12.

1866,
November 3rd.

By indenture of this date made between said Tobias Wrayson, therein described as of Essex Square, in the county of Middlesex, clerk, of one part, and Arthur Shapland, of   , Esq., of other part,

After reciting said policy of assurance and reciting agreement for loan of £2,000 by said Arthur Shapland to said Tobias Wrayson,

It is by abstracting indenture witnessed that in consideration of £2,000 to said Tobias Wrayson paid by said Arthur Shapland, the receipt, &c., said Tobias Wrayson did covenant with said Arthur Shapland to pay £2,000, with interest at £5 per cent., to said Arthur Shapland, his executors, administrators, or assigns on 3rd May then next;

And to pay further interest until principal paid. And it was by abstracting indenture (*inter alia*) further witnessed that in conson of premises, and for further securing payment of said £2,000 and interest, said Tobias Wrayson did assign to said Arthur Shapland, his executors, administrators, and assigns—

All that said recited policy of assurance in the   Life Assurance Company, No. 1,460, and dated 17th May, 1850, and the full benefit thereof. And also said sum of £2,000 thereby assured, and all other monies and sums which should under regulations of said company be appropriated by way of bonus to said policy;

Together with power for said Arthur Shapland, his executors, administrators, or assigns, in the name or names of said Tobias Wrayson, his executors or administrators or otherwise, to sue for, recover, and give receipts for such monies or any part thereof,

To hold and receive said policy, monies, and premises thereby assigned unto and by said Arthur Shapland, his executors, administrators, and assigns.

Proviso for redemption and re-assignment of said policy, monies, and premises, on payment by said Tobias Wrayson, his executors, administrators, or assigns, to said Arthur Shapland, his executors, administrators, or assigns, of £2,000 with interest at £5 per cent., on 3rd May then next.

ABSTRACT No. 12.

Usual mortgage covenants.

Power of sale.

Declaration that the receipts in writing of said Arthur Shapland, his executors, administrators, or assigns, for any money which he or they might receive by virtue of or under the policy of assurance thereby assigned, or for any money payable to him or them under or by virtue of abstracting indenture, should discharge the person or persons, assurance company, or society or societies, paying the same, therefrom, and from all responsibility of seeing to the application thereof, and from being answerable for any loss, misapplication, or nonapplication thereof, and that no person or society paying any such money should be bound to inquire whether any money remained due on the security of abstracting indenture.

      Executed by said Tobias Wrayson,
      and attested.

      Receipt for £2,000 endorsed, signed by said Tobias Wrayson, and witnessed.

The following Notice of said Mortgage was given in duplicate to the   Life Assurance Company:

"Gentlemen,—You will be pleased to take notice that by an indenture of mortgage, dated the 3rd day of November, 1866, and made between the Reverend Tobias Wrayson, of, &c., clerk, of the one part, and Arthur Shapland, of, &c., Esq., of the other part, a certain instrument or policy of assurance, numbered 1,460, under the hands and seals of three of the directors of the   Life Assurance Company, whereby the sum of £2,000 was assured to be paid to the executors, administrators, or assigns of the said Tobias Wrayson, on satisfactory proof of his death, was (with any bonus thereon), for the consideration in the said indenture expressed, assigned to the said Arthur Shapland, his executors, administrators, and assigns. And that the said instrument or policy of assurance was thereupon duly handed over and delivered to the said Arthur

Shapland, who now holds and retains the same. Dated this 4th day of November, 1866.

      "I am your obedient Servant,

         "A—— B——,

     "Solicitor for said Arthur Shapland.

"To the Directors of the
   " Life Assurance Company.

"P.S.—You will please to direct that all future notices, &c., relative to the above policy, may be sent to Mr. Shapland at the above address."

The notice in duplicate was accompanied with the following letter:—

    "Policy No. 1,460.

"Sir,—Herewith I beg to forward duplicate notices of assignment by way of mortgage of the above policy in your office, from Reverend Mr. Wrayson to Mr. Shapland.

"Be pleased to enter the notice in your books, and return one of the notices to me with an endorsement thereon that a duplicate thereof has been received.

       "I am, &c.,

         "A—— B——.

"To , Esq., Actuary, or Secretary,
    " Life Office."

1868,
January 23rd. Probate copy will of said Arthur Shapland, whereby he gave to his wife Louisa Shapland all his personal estate, and appointed her sole executrix of his will.

      Signed by said testator,
     and attested by two witnesses.

1870,
May 9th. Said Arthur Shapland died.

1870,
June 21st. Said will duly proved by said Louisa Shapland in Her Majesty's Court of Probate at Principal Registry.

1870,
July 29th. Said Tobias Wrayson died intestate.

ABSTRACT No. 12.

Letters of administration of personal estate of said Tobias Wrayson granted to Marianne Wrayson, his widow and relict, by Her Majesty's Court of Probate at Principal Registry.   1870, September 1st.

On the death of the assured the policy becomes a claim.

On the 10th September, 1870, Messrs. M. & O. (the solicitors acting for Mrs. Marianne Wrayson) wrote a letter to the actuary of the insurance office giving notice of the death of the assured, and making a claim to the £2,000 assured and bonus.

Mrs. Louisa Shapland sent the following letter to the company:—

"To the Directors of the   Life Assurance Company.

"Policy, No. 1,460.

"Gentlemen,—With reference to a notice served upon you, and acknowledged the 7th of November, 1866, I now beg to claim payment of the sum due on your policy, No. 1,460, £2,000 and bonus, on the life of the late Reverend Tobias Wrayson, who died at   on the 29th July last.

"I enclose certificate of the medical gentleman who attended Mr. Wrayson during his last illness, also certificates of the death and burial of Mr. Wrayson.

"The assignment of your policy to my late husband, and the probate of my late husband's will, and also the policy, will be ready for the inspection of your solicitor.

"I am, &c.

"To   Esq.,
"Actuary or Secretary."

No. 13.

FREEHOLD TITLE.—Abstract of title to a Freehold farm and estate, called Oak Tree Farm, situate in the parish of O——, in the county of R——, as to entirety of said estate.

1807,
November 29th

By indenture of feoffment of this date, made between Thomas Mantell of the first part, Isaac Dayrell, of, &c., of the second part, Robert Lydford, of, &c., of third part, and William Scott of fourth part,

It is witnessed that, in consideration of £4,000 paid by said Isaac Dayrell and Robert Lydford (in equal shares) to said Thomas Mantell, at or before, &c., the receipt, &c., and in consideration of ten shillings to said Thomas Mantell paid by said William Scott, said Thomas Mantell did grant, enfeoff, and confirm to said William Scott and his heirs—

> All that messuage, farm-house, or tenement, with the yards, gardens, orchards, outbuildings, and appurtenances, and the several closes, pieces, or parcels of arable, meadow, pasture, and woodland therewith occupied and enjoyed, containing by estimation 200 acres, more or less, and commonly called or known by the name of Oak Tree Farm, and being situate and lying in the parish of O——, in the county of R——, and then in the occupation of said Thomas Mantell, and which several closes and premises were then known by the several names of, &c., &c. [set out names of fields],
>
> Together, &c., and reversion, &c., and all estate, &c.

Scott, Feoffee to uses.

To hold same to said William Scott and his heirs,

To uses following (that is to say):—

As to one moiety.

As to, for, and concerning one undivided moiety or equal half-part of said messuage, lands, and premises (the whole into two equal parts being considered as divided),

To use of Isaac Dayrell in fee simple.

To the use of said Isaac Dayrell, his heirs and assigns, for ever.

ABSTRACT No. 13.

And as to, for, and concerning the other equal undivided moiety of said messuage, lands, and premises, thereby enfeoffed and conveyed, — *As to other moiety.*

> To the use of said Robert Lydford, his heirs and assigns, for ever. — *To use of Robert Lydford in fee simple.*

Covenants by said Thomas Mantell with said William Scott, that he was lawfully seized, had power to convey, for peaceable possession, freedom from incumbrances, and for further assurance.

>> Executed by said Thomas Mantell, and attested.

>> Receipt for £4,000 endorsed, signed by said Thomas Mantell, and witnessed.

Memorandum of livery of seizin endorsed.

As to Dayrell's Moiety.

Probate copy will of said Isaac Dayrell, therein described as of   , in the county of   , whereby said testator bequeathed all his personal estate to his wife, Maria Dayrell, and appointed her sole executrix of his will. — *1824, May 4th.*

And said testator gave and devised—

> All his messuages, farms, lands, and freehold estates, and parts and shares of real estates (including his moiety of the Oak Tree Farm, situate in the parish of O——, in the county of R——,

To the use of testator's said wife, Maria Dayrell, and her assigns, during her life . . . . . . remainder. — *To use of wife, Maria Dayrell, for her life . . . . remainder.*

To use of testator's son, William Dayrell, and the heirs male of his body . . . . remainder. — *To use of testator's son, William Dayrell, in tail male . . . . . remainder.*

To use of testator's son, Joseph Dayrell, and the heirs of his body lawfully issuing . . . remainder. — *To use of testator's son, Joseph Dayrell, in tail general . . . remainder.*

PEDIGREE OF DAYRELL FAMILY.

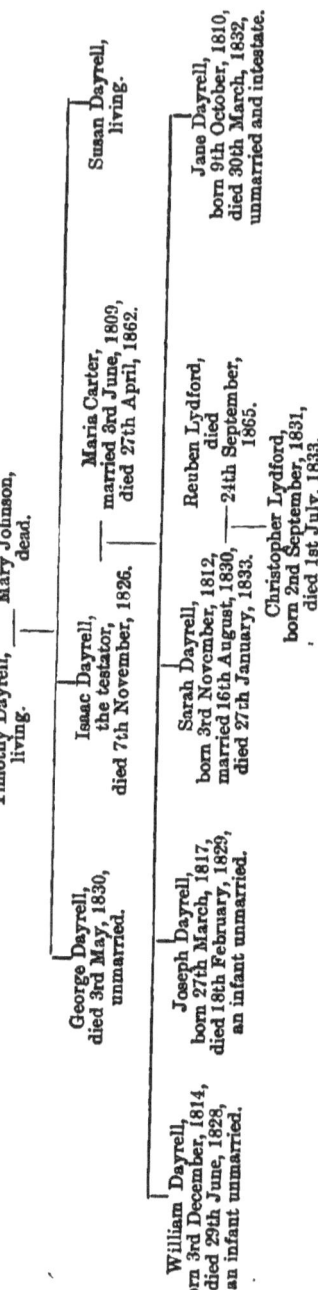

PEDIGREE OF LYDFORD FAMILY.

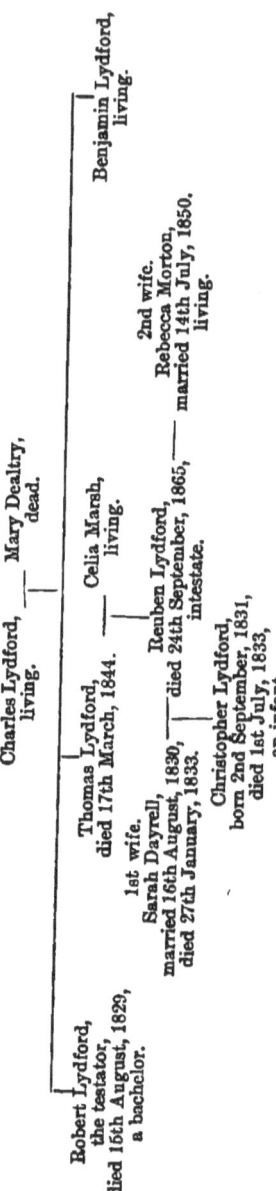

ABSTRACT No. 13.   69

To use of testator's two daughters, Jane Dayrell and Sarah Dayrell, in equal shares, as tenants in common, and to their respective heirs and assigns for ever.   *To use of testator's two daughters Jane Dayrell and Sarah Dayrell, as tenants in common in fee simple.*

Signed by said Isaac Dayrell, and attested by three witnesses.

Said Isaac Dayrell died.   **1826, November 7th.**

His said will proved by said Maria Dayrell, in Consistory Court of Bishop of   .   **1826, December 20th.**

Said William Dayrell died an infant and unmarried.   **1828, June 29th.**

Said Joseph Dayrell died an infant and unmarried.   **1829, February 18th.**

Said Sarah Dayrell married Reuben Lydford.   **1830, August 16th.**

The only issue of this marriage was a son, Christopher Lydford, who was born on 2nd September, 1831.   **1831, September 2nd.**

Said Jane Dayrell died unmarried and intestate.   **1832, March 30th.**

Said Sarah Lydford died.   **1833, January 27th.**

Said Christopher Lydford died.   **1833, July 1st.**

Said Maria Dayrell (widow of Isaac Dayrell) died.   **1862, April 27th.**

Said Reuben Lydford died.   **1865, September 24th.**

AS TO LYDFORD'S MOIETY.

Probate copy will of said Robert Lydford, therein described as of   , in the county of   ,   **1828, April 19th.**
whereby said testator gave and devised—

> All his messuages, lands, and real estates, and shares of estates, and his moiety of Oak Tree Farm, in the parish of O——, in the county of N——, and all his personal estate, unto his nephew, Reuben Lydford (son of testator's brother, Thomas Lydford), his heirs, executors, administrators, and assigns, for ever.

And testator appointed his said nephew Reuben sole executor of his will.

Signed by said testator, and attested by three witnesses.

1829, August 15th.	Said Robert Lydford died.
1829, October 9th.	Said will proved by Reuben Lydford in Consistory Court of Bishop of .
1830, August 16th.	Said Reuben Lydford intermarried with Sarah Dayrell.
1831, September 2nd.	The only issue of this marriage was a son, Christopher Lydford, who was born on 2nd September, 1831.
1833, January 27th.	Said Sarah Lydford (formerly Dayrell) died.
1833, July 1st.	Said Christopher Lydford died, an infant.
1865, September 24th	Said Reuben Lydford died intestate.

On the death of Maria Dayrell (the widow of Isaac Dayrell), on 27th April, 1862, said Reuben Lydford claimed to be entitled to the Dayrell moiety, as tenant, by the courtesy, and entered and continued in possession of the entirety of the estate, until his death, intestate, on 24th September, 1865.

No. 14.

REVERSIONARY INTEREST IN NEW 3 PER CENTS. (STOCK).—
Abstract of the Title of Archer James Rycroft, Esq., and Lucy his wife, to a moiety of a sum of £15,000 Bank £4 per Cent. Annuities (now represented by £15,000 New £3 per Cent. Annuities), under the wills of Sir Gilfred Turville, Bart., and Geoffrey Turville, Esq. (subject to the life interest of Mrs. Miranda Turville).

1830, June 19th. Sir Gilfred Turville, of , Baronet, by his will of this date (Probate copy produced), after directing his executors and trustees to pay his just debts and funeral expenses, and the pecuniary legacies bequeathed by his will,

Gave and bequeathed—

All his stocks, funds, monies, and personal estate and effects whatsoever and wheresoever (except such parts thereof as were thereby specifically bequeathed),

Unto his (testator's) nephew, Geoffrey Turville, and his friends, Arthur Lewis and Matthew Garner, Esqs., their executors, administrators, and assigns,

Upon trust that they, or the survivor of them, should convert into money all such parts of his personal estate as should not consist of money or securities for money; and should thereout, and out of his ready money, pay his funeral and testamentary expenses, and the specific pecuniary legacies thereby bequeathed; and should lay out and invest the residue of such monies in the purchase of such Bank annuities as were therein mentioned (that is to say) (*inter alia*) : in the first place, to purchase £15,000 Bank Four per Cent. Annuities, in the names of his said trustees;

And upon trust to pay the dividends and annual income of such sum of stock, from time to time, when and as the same should be received, unto such person or persons and for such purposes as said testator's daughter, Dame Valeria Sheldon, the wife of Sir Thomas Sheldon, of   , Bart., should by any note in writing under her hand during her life, notwithstanding her then present or any future coverture, and whether she should be covert or sole, direct or appoint; and, subject to and in default of such appointment, into the proper hands of said Dame Valeria Sheldon, for her own sole and separate use and benefit, exclusively of her then present or any future husband; and that the receipt or receipts of said Dame Valeria Sheldon should alone be discharges for such dividends and annual income.

And after the decease of said Dame Valeria Sheldon,

Upon trust that said trustees should stand possessed of said sum of £15,000 £4 per cent. annuities, and the dividends and annual income thereof,

In trust for all and every the children and child of said Dame Valeria Sheldon, equally to be divided between or amongst them (if more than one), share and share alike; and if only one, then

In trust for such one child, to become vested in sons at 21 years of age, and in daughters at that age or day of marriage.

And in case no child of testator's said daughter, Dame Valeria Sheldon, should live to acquire a vested interest in the said sum of £15,000 £4 per Cent. Bank Annuities; or, in case said Dame Valeria Sheldon should not have any child,

Then (after her decease) said sum of £15,000 £4 per Cent. Annuities should fall into and be considered as part of said testator's residuary personal estate.

And as to the ultimate residue of said testator's personal estate, after making such purchases and appropriations as in said will directed and mentioned [these directions should be set out, and it should be shown that they have been satisfied],

Said testator directed his executors and trustees to stand possessed of such ultimate residue,

In trust for his (testator's) nephew, said Geoffrey Turville (as testator's residuary legatee), his executors, administrators, and assigns, absolutely for his own use, and not in his capacity of executor or trustee.

And said testator appointed said Geoffrey Turville, Arthur Lewis, and Matthew Garner, executors and trustees of his said will.

Signed by said Sir Gilfred Turville, and attested by three witnesses.

1832,
November 2nd.   Said Sir Gilfred Turville died.

1832,
December 14th   His said will proved by said Geoffrey Turville, Arthur Lewis, and Matthew Garner, in the Prerogative Court of the Archbishop of Canterbury.

1843,
April 29th.   Said Geoffrey Turville, then of   , Esquire, by his will of this date, after directing payment of his debts, funeral and testamentary expenses, out of his personal estate, and after giving certain specific and pecuniary legacies,

Gave, devised and bequeathed to his executors and trustees thereinafter named, their heirs, executors, administrators and assigns—

> All and singular his real estates, and all his goods, chattels, monies, funds, and personal property, estate, and effects whatsoever (not thereinbefore specifically bequeathed),

To hold same to said trustees, their heirs, executors, administrators, and assigns, upon the trusts, &c., thereinafter expressed, *i.e.*,

Upon trust that said trustees or trustee should convert same premises into money, and invest the same when converted into money, in their or his names or name, in manner therein mentioned.

And upon trust to pay the interest, dividends, and annual income of said trust monies and funds unto Miranda Turville (the wife of said Geoffrey Turville) during her life, for her absolute, sole, and separate use, without power of anticipation.

And after her decease,

Upon trust to transfer, pay, and divide all said trust monies, funds and premises then constituting the residuary personal estate of said testator, and the annual income thereof,

To or in trust for all or any one or more of the children or child, grandchildren, and issue respectively, of said Geoffrey Turville, to be born before any such appointment as thereinafter was mentioned, should be made to them respectively, in such manner and form, and in such parts, shares, and proportions, and at such times, with such limitations over or substitutions in favour of any one or more of the others of his said children, grandchildren, and issue respectively, and either by way of present or remote interest or otherwise, and to vest and be payable and paid upon such contingencies and at such time or times and as to his said grandchildren and more remote issue, under and subject to such directions and regulations for maintenance, education, and advancement, and such conditions and restrictions as testator's said wife, Miranda, notwithstanding her coverture by any future husband, and whether covert or sole, at any time or times, and from time to time, before each and every of his said children should have attained the age of 25 years, or have died under that age, by any deed or deeds, instrument or instruments in writing, to be respectively signed, sealed and delivered by his said wife, in the presence of two or more credible witnesses, and to be attested by the same witnesses, should, either absolutely or with power of revocation and new appointments, such new appointments to be in favour of some one or more of the objects of this present provision, direct, limit, or appoint, and in default of and subject to any such direction, limitation, or appointment,

Upon trust for all and every the children and child of

the said testator, who, being a son or sons, should live to attain the age of 21 years, or, being a daughter or daughters, should attain that age, or marry, and to be divided between them in equal shares as tenants in common.

And the said testator appointed Christopher Gosbell and Martin Fentiman, Esquires, to be executors and trustees of his said will.

Power to appoint new trustees.

Trustees' indemnity clause.

Declaration, trustees' receipts, discharges.

       Signed by said Geoffrey Turville,
       and attested by two witnesses.

1844, March 27th. Said Arthur Lewis died.

1846, September 3rd. Said Matthew Garner died.

1848, March 20th. The said Geoffrey Turville died, leaving said Miranda Turville, his widow, and three children only him surviving, namely, Matthew Turville, Clara Turville, and Lucy Turville.

1848, May 30th. Will of said Geoffrey Turville proved by said Christopher Gosbell and Martin Fentiman in Prerogative Court of Canterbury.

1850, December 7th. By deed poll of appointment of this date, under the hand and seal of said Miranda Turville, widow and relict of said Geoffrey Turville,

> After reciting said abstracted will of said Geoffrey Turville, and his death, and that he left three children him surviving, viz., Matthew Turville, Clara Turville, and Lucy Turville,
>
> And reciting that said Miranda Turville was desirous of exercising by abstracting deed poll the power of appointment so given to her by said abstracted will of said Geoffrey Turville,

It was witnessed that in exercise of the power or authority for that purpose given by said thereinbefore in part recited will, and of every other power or authority enabling her in that behalf, the said Miranda Turville did direct, limit, and appoint that after decease of said Miranda Turville (and subject to her life interest), the said or other the trustees or trustee for the time

ABSTRACT No. 14. 75

being of said recited will of said Geoffrey Turville, should stand possessed of, and pay or assign.

All and singular the trust stocks, securities, funds, and monies then constituting the general residuary personal estate and effects of the said testator, Geoffrey Turville, deceased,

To or in trust for the said Clara Turville and Lucy Turville, equally to be divided between them, share and share alike, as tenants in common, and their respective executors, administrators, and assigns.

Proviso and declaration that it should be lawful for her, said Miranda Turville, at any time or times thereafter, by any deed or deeds, instrument or instruments in writing, to be signed, sealed, and delivered by her in the presence of and attested by two or more credible witnesses, to revoke and make void all and every or any of the trusts, intents, purposes and provisions thereinbefore directed, limited, and appointed, of and concerning the aforesaid general residuary funds, monies, and estate, or any part or parts thereof; and by the same deed or deeds, instrument or instruments in writing, or in and by any other deed or deeds, instrument or instruments in writing, to be signed, sealed and delivered and attested as aforesaid, to declare, direct and appoint any new or other trust or trusts, powers, provisions, or purposes, of or concerning the same general residuary estate, monies, and funds, or any part or parts thereof, in such manner as to the said Miranda Turville should seem meet.

Executed by said Miranda Turville, and attested by two witnesses.

The said Dame Valeria Sheldon died without having had a child. 1866, February 3rd.

Statutory declaration as to her death without having had any child :— 1872, January 17th.

I, Maria Glanville, of , in the county of , widow, do solemnly and sincerely declare as follows (that is to say) :

1. I am one of the daughters of Sir Gilfred Turville, late of , Baronet, who died on the 2nd day of November, 1832.

ABSTRACT No. 14.

2. I well knew Dame Valeria Sheldon, the wife of Sir Thomas Sheldon, of   , in the county of   , Bart., she being my sister, and one of the daughters of the said Sir Gilfred Turville.

3. The said Dame Valeria Sheldon died on the 3rd day of February, 1866, and is the same person as the "Lady Valeria Sheldon, wife of Sir Thomas Sheldon," mentioned in the certificate or paper writing now produced and shown to me, marked A.

4. My said sister, the said Dame Valeria Sheldon, was only once married, and never had any child.

And I make this solemn declaration, &c.

1860,
May 31st.

By deed poll of this date, under hand and seal of said Miranda Turville (indorsed on said abstracted deed poll of 7th December, 1859),

Reciting that said Miranda Turville had not at any time or in any manner exercised the power of revocation and new appointment given and reserved to her by the thereinwithin written deed poll of revoking and altering the appointment thereby made, of and concerning the trust, monies, funds, and premises thereby appointed;

And reciting that it was the determination of the said Miranda Turville not in any manner to exercise such power of revocation and new appointment, and that the appointment made by such deed poll in favour of the said Clara Turville and Lucy Turville should be absolute and irrevocable; and with the view and intention of making such appointment absolute, the said Miranda Turville had agreed and intended wholly and absolutely to release same trust, monies, funds and premises from the aforesaid power of revocation and new appointment,

It is by the abstracting deed poll witnessed that, in pursuance of said agreement and intention, and for divers good causes, said Miranda Turville did thereby release and for ever discharge

All and singular the trust stocks, securities, funds, monies, general residuary personal estates and effects of the said Geoffrey Turville, the testator, deceased, appointed by the thereinwithin written deed poll,

Of and from the said power of revocation and new

appointment thereby given or reserved to said Miranda Turville;

To the end, intent, and purpose that the appointment made by the thereinwithin written deed poll in favour of the said Clara Turville and Lucy Turville might be absolute and irrevocable, and that all and singular the said trust stocks, securities, funds, monies, and general residuary estate, and every part thereof, might thenceforth be discharged and exonerated from the said power of revocation and new appointment, and that the said Miranda Turville might be barred and absolutely excluded from exercising the same.

Executed by said Miranda Turville,
and attested by two witnesses.

Said Lucy Turville intermarried with Archer James Rycroft, at the parish church of St.   .

1869,
October 29th.

No. 15.

POLICY OF LIFE ASSURANCE.—Equitable Mortgage by Deposit. Administration Suit.

Abstract of Title of Mrs. Caroline Holcombe (as executrix of will of Jasper Holcombe) to a Policy of Assurance for £5,000 payable on the death of Jasper Holcombe (a claim).

By an instrument or policy of assurance of this date, No. 2,462, under the hands and seals of three of the directors of the   Life Assurance Company,

1860,
June 28th.

The sum of £5,000 was assured to be paid to the executors, administrators, or assigns of Jasper Holcombe, of No.   Street, in the parish of   , in the county of   , Esquire, within six months after proof of the death of the said Jasper Holcombe.

Subject, nevertheless, to the payment of the yearly premium of £   during the life of the said Jasper Holcombe, and to the observance and performance of certain conditions, stipulations, and agreements in the said policy mentioned or referred to.

Executed by three directors of said Company and attested.

Memorandum of Deposit of Deeds and Policy with Bankers.

1868,
October 9th.

This memorandum of deposit has an *ad valorem* stamp of £2 10s.

This is a full copy of the memorandum of deposit.

Memorandum.—I, Jasper Holcombe, of   , in the county of   , Esquire, do hereby admit and declare that I have this day deposited with Messrs. A. B. and Company, of   , in the county of   , Bankers, the deeds, shares, and policies of Life Assurance mentioned in the schedule hereunder written, which deeds, shares, and policies are to be held and retained by them and their partners for the time being, by way of a continuing security to them for securing payment to them on demand of all sums of money and liabilities already advanced, paid, or incurred, or which they or any of them, or any of their partners for the time being, may at any time advance, pay, or incur to or for me, or for my use, or on my account, whether on current account or by the discount of or otherwise in respect of bills of exchange, promissory notes, cheques, or other negociable securities drawn, accepted, or indorsed by me, or by way of loan to me, together with interest, commission, banking charges, law and other costs, charges, and expenses; and for the purpose of making a more effectual security for such several sums, monies, and matters, above mentioned, I hereby undertake and agree, at my own costs and expenses, in all respects, when requested by the said Messrs. A. B. and Company, that I and all other necessary parties will execute and deliver to them, or as they shall direct and require, a legal and effectual mortgage (duly stamped) of all my estate and interest in the freehold estate, policies, shares, and premises comprised in the said deeds, policies, and shares, which mortgage shall contain a power of sale and all usual and requisite covenants and clauses as the counsel of the said bankers shall direct and require, and this security shall be applicable and extend as well to my separate account current and my loan account (separate) and separate liability as to any joint current or loan account, or

ABSTRACT No. 15.

liabilities with any other person or persons as partner or partners or otherwise. Witness my hand this 9th day of October, 1868.

    (Signed)   JASPER HOLCOMBE.

Signed in the presence of

The schedule above referred to contains the before abstracted policy of assurance (*inter alia*).   1860, June 28th.

Notice of said abstracted memorandum of deposit was given by the solicitor of the bankers to insurance office.   1868, October 9th.

Probate copy will of said Jasper Holcombe, whereby he gave and bequeathed   1870, July 26th.

> All his personal estate and effects whatsoever and wheresoever unto his wife Caroline Holcombe, for her absolute benefit, subject to the payment thereout of testator's debts and funeral and testamentary expenses.

And he appointed his said wife sole executrix of his will.

    Signed by said testator, and
    attested by two witnesses.

Said Jasper Holcombe died.   1871, November 4th.

Said will proved by said Caroline Holcombe in Her Majesty's Court of Probate at Principal Registry.   1872, March 23rd.

Bill filed in High Court of Chancery, in which Thomas Peters was Plaintiff and said Caroline Holcombe was Defendant.   1872, March 29th.

After stating (*inter alia*) a certain indenture of mortgages of a certain freehold estate from said Jasper Holcombe to said Thomas Peters for securing £9,000 and interest.

The prayer of said Bill was (*inter alia*)—

1. That an account might be decreed to be taken under the authority of said Court of what was due to the Plaintiff and the other unsatisfied creditors of said Jasper Holcombe for principal and interest.

2. That the real and personal estates of said testator

might be applied in a due course of administration under direction of said Court.

1872,
May 14th.

By an order made in said Cause, it was (*inter alia*) ordered that the following accounts and inquiry be taken and made, that is to say (*inter alia*)—
1. An account of what was due to the Plaintiff and all other the creditors of said Jasper Holcombe, the testator in the Bill named.
2. An account of the testator's funeral expenses.
3. An account of the testator's personal estate come to the hands of the Defendant, the executrix, or to the hands of any other person or persons by or for her order or use.
4. An inquiry what parts (if any) of the testator's personal estate were outstanding or undisposed of.

And it was ordered that the testator's personal estate be applied in payment of his debts and funeral expenses in a due course of administration.

Further consideration adjourned.

No. 16.

LEASEHOLD FOR YEARS.—Abstract of the Title of Mrs. Martha Harton to ten Leasehold messuages and gardens, known as Nos. 1 to 10 inclusive, in Augusta Square, in the parish of St.   , in the county of Middlesex.

1830,
July 1st.

By indenture of lease of this date, made between Arthur Latimer, of, &c., Esq., of the one part, and Robert Chard, of, &c., builder, of other part,
It is witnessed that in consideration of the rent and covenants thereinafter reserved and contained, and on the part of said Robert Chard to be paid and performed, said Arthur Latimer did grant, demise, and lease to said Robert Chard, his executors, administrators, and assigns—
All that piece or parcel of land or ground, situate

ABSTRACT No. 16.

in the parish of St.   , in the county of Middlesex, bounded on the north by the   Road, and on all other sides by other ground belonging to said Arthur Latimer, and containing the several dimensions set forth on the plan drawn in the margin of abstracting indenture of lease, and therein coloured pink,

With the appurtenances;

To hold said premises to said Robert Chard, his executors, administrators, and assigns, for the term of ninety-nine years, to be computed from 24th June then last past, at and under the yearly rent of £50, payable quarterly on the four most usual quarterly days of payment, and the first quarterly payment to be made on 29th day of September then next ensuing.

Covenants by said Robert Chard:
To pay said rent.
To pay all rates and taxes.
To build and complete ten messuages on said piece of ground.
To keep in repair.
To surrender same at end of term.
To insure messuages and buildings in £4,000, in names of lessor and lessee.
To rebuild in case of fire.
Not to assign said lease, or part with possession of said ground or premises, without license and consent, in writing, of said Arthur Latimer, his heirs or assigns, first had and obtained.

Proviso for re-entry on non-payment of rent, or non-performance of covenants by lessee.

Covenant by lessor for quiet enjoyment.

    Executed by said Arthur Latimer,
      and attested.

Registered in Middlesex, 17th August, 1830.
 B.   , No.   .

Ten messuages were built on said piece of ground which now forms part of Augusta Square; the houses are numbered 1 to 10 in Augusta Square.

By indenture of this date, made between said Robert   1856,
                  June 14th.

Chard, of first part, William Wood, of, &c. (the official assignee of the estate and effects of said Robert Chard under a fiat in Bankruptcy), of second part, Thomas James, of, &c., and Richard Williams, of, &c. (the creditors' assignees under said fiat), of the third part, and Thomas Parker, of, &c., of fourth part,

> Reciting said abstracted indenture of lease of 1st July, 1830, and that said Robert Chard had built ten messuages on said piece of ground comprised in said lease;
> And reciting that on 3rd May, 1856, a petition for adjudication in Bankruptcy was filed against said Robert Chard, and on the 14th day of same month he was declared and adjudged to be a bankrupt by the Court of Bankruptcy in London;
> And reciting that said William Wood was duly appointed official assignee of the estate and effects of said bankrupt, and said Thomas James and Richard Williams were, on the 24th day of May, 1856, duly appointed creditors' assignees of the estate and effects of said bankrupt;
> And reciting that said parties to abstracting indenture of third part (as such creditors' assignees as aforesaid) caused said piece of ground and ten messuages comprised in said lease to be put up for sale by public auction on the   day of   , at the Auction Mart, in the City of London, according to certain printed particulars and conditions of sale then and there produced, and that at the same sale said Thomas Parker became the highest bidder for, and was declared the purchaser of, said piece of ground and ten messuages comprised in said lease, at the price of £4,500;

It is by said abstracting indenture witnessed that, for completing said sale and in consideration of £4,500 to said William Wood (as such official assignee as aforesaid) paid by said Thomas Parker, the receipt, &c., they, the said William Wood, Thomas James, and Richard Williams (as such assignees respectively as aforesaid) did grant and assign, and said Robert Chard did grant, assign, and confirm to said Thomas Parker—

> All that said piece of ground and premises com-

prised in and demised by said abstracted indenture of lease,

And also all those the several ten messuages or tenements which had been erected upon, and were then standing on, said piece of ground, and were then known as Nos. 1 to 10 inclusive in Augusta Square,

Together with appurtenances,

And all estate, &c., of said parties of first, second, and third parts;

To hold said premises to said Thomas Parker, his executors, administrators, and assigns, during all residue then to come of said term of ninety-nine years, created by said abstracted indenture of lease of 1st July, 1830, subject to payment of said rent of £50 and to performance of lessee's covenants.

Covenant by said parties thereto of first and second parts that they had not incumbered.

Covenants by said Robert Chard :
   That lease was a valid and subsisting lease.
   That rent and covenants had been paid and performed up to   day of   last.
   That parties of first, second, and third parts had power to assign.
   For peaceable possession.
   Freedom from incumbrances.
   And further assurance.

Covenant by said Thomas Parker for payment of rent and performance of covenants.

                        Executed by all parties, and attested.

Probate copy will of said Thomas Parker, whereby (*inter alia*) said testator gave and bequeathed   **1856, December 9th.**
   To his niece, Maria Watson, an annuity of £100 during her life.
   And to his (testator's) sister, Clara Parker, an annuity of £100 during her life.

And testator charged all his leasehold houses and property in Augusta Square with payment of said annuities.

And, subject to payment of said annuities thereby given, said testator bequeathed—

All his said leasehold estates, messuages, and hereditaments, and all the residue of his personal estate and effects, unto his son, Matthew Parker, absolutely during all testator's term and interest therein at the time of his death.

And said testator appointed his said son, Matthew Parker, sole executor of his said will.

Signed by said Thomas Parker,
and attested by two witnesses.

1856, December 27th. Said Thomas Parker died.

1857, February 8th. Said will of said Thomas Parker proved by said Matthew Parker in Prerogative Court of Canterbury.

1864, April 24th. Probate copy will of said Matthew Parker, whereby said testator gave and bequeathed—

All his leasehold estates and property, and all other his personal estate and effects whatsoever, unto his sister, Martha Harton (the wife of Jacob Harton, of, &c.), for her sole and separate use, benefit, and disposal, and her receipts alone to be sufficient discharges for same.

And testator revoked all former wills and appointed his said sister, Martha Harton, sole executrix of his said will.

1868, November 17th. Said Matthew Parker died.

1869, May 1st. Said will of said Matthew Parker proved by said Martha Harton in Her Majesty's Court of Probate, at Principal Registry.

The title of the lessor, Arthur Latimer, not to be required to be shown.

No. 17.

FREEHOLD TITLE.—Abstract of the Title of Mr. Frederick Parkes and others to a messuage, farm, and Freehold estate, called Morton's, situate in the parish of N——, in the county of S——.

By indenture of lease of this date, made between John Watson, of , in the county of , of the one part, and Robert Parkes, of , of the other part,

1780,
March 24th.

It is witnessed that in consideration of the natural love and affection which the said John Watson had for his grandson, the said Robert Parkes, the said John Watson did grant and demise to the said Robert Parkes, his executors, administrators, and assigns—

> All that messuage, farm, and lands commonly called or known by the name of Mortons, containing by estimation 170 acres or thereabouts, situate, lying, and being in the parish of N——, in the county of S——, and being then in the tenure or occupation of the said Robert Parkes, and being bounded on the east by the river or brook called

To hold same unto said Robert Parkes, his executors, administrators, and assigns, from the day next before the day of the date of the indenture now in rental for the term of 999 years thence next ensuing,

> Yielding and paying yearly and every year during the said term unto the said John Watson, his heirs, or assigns, the yearly rent of £5, by equal half-yearly payments on the 29th day of September and 25th day of March.

Covenants by said Robert Parkes:
For payment of said rent and all taxes, &c.
For due cultivation of said farm.

Executed by said John Watson, and attested.

ABSTRACT No. 17.

1830,
June 18th.

By indenture of this date made between Edward Parkes, of   , in the county of   , of the one part, and Charles Taylor, of   , in the county of   , of the other part,

After reciting said abstracted lease of 24th March, 1780,

And reciting that under and by virtue of divers mesne assignments, and other acts in law, said messuage, farm, and estate comprised in said abstracted lease, had become vested in said Edward Parkes during residue of said term of 999 years;

And reciting that it was not known who was then entitled to the reversion of the said messuage, farm, and lands;

And reciting that with a view to acquire the freehold and inheritance of and in the said messuage, farm, and hereditaments comprised in said recited indenture of lease by an indenture of feoffment, then already prepared and engrossed, and intended to bear date the day next after the day of the date of the now abstracting indenture, and to be made between the said Edward Parkes, of the first part, Thomas Chard, of the second part, and A. B., of the third part, and on which livery of seizin was intended to be given and endorsed, the said Edward Parkes did intend to grant and enfeoff unto the said Thomas Chard and his heirs the same messuage, farm, and estate comprised in and granted and demised by the said reindented indorse of lease of the 24th day of March, 1780, with the appurtenances by the modern description of all that, &c., to hold the same unto the said Thomas Chard and his heirs. To the uses and in manner thereinafter mentioned.

And that with a view to strengthen the title to the said hereditaments and premises, the said Edward Parkes, by the same indorse of feoffment, did intend to covenant to levy a fine, sur conuzance de droit come ceo, &c., with proclamations of the said messuage, hereditaments, and premises.

And that it was by the said indenture of feoffment intended to be declared that the said feoffment and fine should enure to such uses and upon such trusts as the said Edward Parkes by any deed or deeds, with or without power of revocation and new appointment, should appoint. And in default of and until and subject to such appointment, to the use of the said Edward Parkes, his heirs and assigns for ever;

And reciting that the said Edward Parkes was desirous that previously to the execution of the said indenture of feoffment, the said messuage, hereditaments, and premises, comprised in the said abstracted indenture of lease of 24th March, 1780, should be assigned to a trustee for the remainder of the said term of 999 years upon the trusts thereinafter declared concerning the same;

It was by abstracting indenture witnessed, that in pursuance of said desire, and in consideration of 10s. to said Edward Parkes paid by said Charles Taylor at or before, &c., the receipt, &c., said Edward Parkes did grant, bargain, sell, and assign unto said Charles Taylor, his executors, administrators, and assigns—

> The said messuage, lands, and hereditaments, and all other the premises comprised in and demised by the thereinbefore recited indenture of lease of 24th March, 1780, with the appurtenances and all the estate, &c.

To hold same unto said Charles Taylor, his executors, administrators, and assigns, during all residue then to come of said term of 999 years,

> In trust for said Edward Parkes, his executors, administrators, and assigns, until said then intended indenture of feoffment should be duly executed and perfected. And immediately after the execution and perfecting of the same indenture of feoffment,
> In trust for said Edward Parkes, his heirs, appointees, and assigns. And from time to time to assign and dispose of the same term as he or they should direct or appoint. And in the mean time,
> In trust to permit the said term to attend and wait upon the freehold and inheritance which should be acquired of the said messuage, lands, heredi-

taments, and premises, by or by means of the said intended indenture of feoffment and fine, and to protect the same from all mesne incumbrances (if any such there should be).

Executed by said Edward Parkes and Charles Taylor, and attested.

1880,
June 19th.

Indenture of feoffment of this date made between said Edward Parkes, of first part, Thomas Chard, of second part, and A. B., of third part,

Reciting that said Edward Parkes was desirous of making a feoffment and levying a fine of the messuage and other hereditaments hereinafter described, and intended to be thereby granted and enfeoffed with the appurtenances to the uses thereinafter declared concerning the same.

It is by the indenture now abstracting witnessed, that in consideration of the sum of ten shillings of lawful monies, &c., by said Thomas Chard to said Edward Parkes, paid at or before, &c., the receipt, &c., said Edward Parkes did give, grant, enfeoff and confirm unto said Thomas Chard and his heirs,

All that messuage, &c. (premises comprised in said abstracted lease of 24th March, 1780).
And reversion, &c.
And all estate, &c.

To hold same hereditaments and premises with their appurtenances unto said Thomas Chard and his heirs,

To the uses and upon the trusts, and with, under, and subject to the power thereinafter declared concerning same.

And for further assuring to the uses and in manner thereinafter mentioned, said messuage, lands, and hereditaments, thereby granted and enfeoffed or intended so to be, and for corroborating, strengthening, and confirming the title thereto, said Edward Parkes did covenant with said Thomas Chard and his heirs that said Edward Parkes would in or as of then present Trinity Term levy unto said Thomas Chard and his heirs one or more fine or fines, sur conuzance de droit come ceo, &c., of said messuage, lands, and premises.

ABSTRACT No. 17. 89

Declaration that said grant and enfeoffment thereinbefore contained, and said fine, &c., should operate and enure,
> To such uses and upon such trusts, &c., as said Edward Parkes should by any deed, &c., appoint, and in default of such appointment, to use of said Edward Parkes, his heirs and assigns, for ever.
>> Executed by said Edward Parkes and Thomas Chard, and attested.

Livery of seizin endorsed on last abstracted indenture.

Chirograph indentures of fine between Thomas Chard, plaintiff, and Edward Parkes, deforceant, of— *(Trinity Term, 11th Geo. 4th.)*
> Two messuages, two stables, two barns, two gardens, two orchards, two hundred acres of land, one hundred acres of meadow, one hundred acres of pasture, with the appurtenances, in the parish of N——.

Delivered with proclamations.

Probate copy will of said Edward Parkes, whereby said testator gave, and devised, and appointed— *1838, January 29th.*
> All his freehold messuages, lands, and hereditaments, and all his real estates,

unto his three sons, Frederick Parkes, Jeremiah Parkes, and Rowland Parkes, their heirs and assigns, for ever, in equal shares as tenants in common and not as joint tenants.

And testator appointed his eldest son, Frederick Parkes, executor of his said will.
>> Signed by said Edward Parkes, and attested by three witnesses.

Said Edward Parkes died. *1839, October 4th.*

Said will proved by said Frederick Parkes in Consistory Court of Bishop of . *1839, December 10th*

As to One-third of Jeremiah Parkes.

1840,
June 27th
& 28th.

Indentures of lease and release between said Jeremiah Parkes, of first part, Charlotte Benson, of, &c., spinster, of second part, and Thomas Thorpe of, &c., of third part,

> Reciting said abstracted will of said Edward Parkes.
>
> And reciting that marriage then intended between said Jeremiah Parkes and Charlotte Benson.
>
> And agreement that said one-third of said Jeremiah Parkes should be conveyed and settled to uses, &c., thereinafter expressed.

It was by abstracting indenture of release witnessed, that in consideration of said intended marriage, and of ten shillings paid to him by said Thomas Thorpe, said Jeremiah Parkes, with approbation of said Charlotte Benson (testified, &c.), did grant, release, and confirm unto said Thomas Thorpe (in his actual possession then being, &c.) and his heirs—

> All that the one undivided third part or share (the whole into three equal parts or shares being considered as divided) of him, said Jeremiah Parkes, of and in
>
> All that messuage, tenement, or farm-house, with the barns, stables, outbuildings, and appurtenances, and the several closes, pieces, or parcels of land, held, used, and occupied therewith, containing one hundred and seventy acres or thereabouts by estimation, and being called or known by the name of   , and being situate and being in the parish of N——, in the county of S——, formerly in the occupation of said Edward Parkes, and then of said Frederick Parkes or his under-tenants, and which estate was devised by said will of said Edward Parkes as aforesaid. And of and in all houses, &c., reversions, &c., and all estate, &c.;

To hold same one-third part and premises unto said Thomas Thorpe and his heirs,

> To uses thereinafter expressed and limited (*i.e.*) to

use of said Jeremiah Parkes and his heirs until solemnization of said then intended marriage; and after solemnization thereof,

To use of said Jeremiah Parkes and his assigns during his life . . . . remainder.
To use of said Charlotte Benson and her assigns during her life . . . . remainder.
To use of the issue of the body of said Jeremiah Parkes by said Charlotte Benson, in equal shares; and in default of such issue,
To the use of said Jeremiah Parkes, his heirs and assigns for ever.

> Executed by said Jeremiah Parkes and Charlotte Benson, and attested.

Said marriage solemnized between said Jeremiah Parkes and Charlotte Benson at parish church of . **1840, June 29th.**

The issue of said marriage were—

Rupert Parkes, born 28th August, 1841.
James Parkes, born 7th September, 1843.
Francis Parkes, born 18th March, 1845.

As to One-third of Rowland Parkes.

Probate copy will of said Rowland Parkes, whereby said testator gave and devised— **1848, January 17th.**

All his messuages, lands, and freehold estates and shares of real estates whatsoever—

unto his brother, Jeremiah Parkes, and his children, in equal shares.

And he appointed his brother, Jeremiah Parkes, sole executor of his said will.

> Signed by said Rowland Parkes, and attested by two witnesses.

Said Rowland Parkes died a bachelor. **1849, May 4th.**

His said will proved by said Jeremiah Parkes in Consistorial Court of Bishop of   . **1849, June 23rd.**

1860,
April 27th.
Probate copy will of said Jeremiah Parkes, whereby testator gave and devised—

>All his freehold and real estates whatsoever and wheresoever, and all his personal estate,
unto his wife Charlotte Parkes, her heirs, executors, administrators, and assigns, for ever, for her own use, and appointed her sole executrix of his will.

>>Signed by testator,
and attested by two witnesses.

1868,
October 30th.
Said Jeremiah Parkes died.

1869,
January 4th.
His will proved by said Charlotte Parkes in Her Majesty's Court of Probate, District Registry of

>Frederick Parkes,
Charlotte Parkes,
Rupert Parkes,   } are all living.
James Parkes,
Francis Parkes,

No. 18.

Reversionary Interest in Bank Shares and Railway Debentures.

SPEARTON'S TITLE.—Abstract of the Title of the next of kin of Miss Margaretta Spearton to 40 Shares of £100 each in L—— and W—— Bank, and £4,000 East Indian Railway Debentures (being part of the residuary personal estate of Mr. Basil Welford, deceased), subject to the life interest of Mrs. Frances Welford.

1866,
March 11th.
Probate copy of will of Basil Welford, of   ,
Esq., whereby, after giving several specific and pecuniary legacies,

>The testator gave and bequeathed his 40 shares in

the L—— and W—— Bank, then standing in
the joint names of Robert Spearton, of   ,
Esq., and testator's brother, Raymond Welford
(in trust for testator), and £4,000 East Indian
railway debentures then standing in same names,
in trust for testator, and all the rest and residue
of testator's personal estate unto said Robert
Spearton and Raymond Welford upon trust, to
invest residuary personal estate as in said will
expressed (after payment of testator's debts and
funeral and testamentary expenses and the pecuniary legacies bequeathed by his will);

And upon trust to pay the interest, dividends, and annual income of said 40 shares in L—— and W—— Bank, and of said £4,000 East Indian railway debentures, and of all other testator's residuary personal estate,

Unto said testator's wife, Frances Welford, and her assigns, during her life; and after her death,

Said testator directed said shares and debentures, and all other his residuary personal estate, and the income thereof, to be held by his trustees and executors,

In trust for testator's nephew, Charles Welford, if and when and in case he should live to attain the age of 21 years. But in case said Charles Welford should die under the age of 21 years,

Then (immediately after his decease) as to the capital and income of said 40 shares in L—— and W—— Bank, and £4,000 East Indian railway debentures, and all other the testator's residuary personal estate,

In trust for said Robert Spearton, his executors and administrators, for his and their absolute benefit.

Power for said Frances Welford during her life to appoint a new trustee or new trustees for purposes of said will.

And said testator appointed said Robert Spearton and Raymond Welford executors of his said will.

Signed by said testator, Basil Welford,
and attested by two witnesses.

Said Basil Welford died.   1866,
                                                                November 24th

ABSTRACT No. 18.

1867,
January 7th.
Said will proved by said Robert Spearton and Raymond Welford in Her Majesty's Court of Probate at Principal Registry.

1868,
August 27th.
Probate copy will of said Robert Spearton, whereby, after directing his funeral and testamentary expenses and debts to be paid by his executors,

The testator bequeathed all the residue and remainder of his personal estate and effects whatsoever unto Peter Langham, of   , and Moses Penton, of   , their executors and administrators,

Upon trust to stand possessed of his said residuary personal estate,

In trust for testator's niece, Margaretta Spearton (the daughter of testator's late brother, Samuel Spearton) her executors and administrators absolutely.

And testator appointed said Peter Langham and Moses Penton executors of his said will.

Signed by said Robert Spearton,
and attested by two witnesses.

1869,
September 19th
Said Robert Spearton died.

1869,
October 23rd.
Will of said Robert Spearton proved by both said executors in Her Majesty's Court of Probate at Principal Registry.

1870,
June 9th.
By indenture of this date made between said Frances Welford of 1st part, said Raymond Welford of 2nd part, and Richard Clare, of   , in county of   , of 3rd part, after reciting said will of said Basil Welford and his death and proof of his will, and reciting death of said Robert Spearton, it is by abstracting indenture witnessed that said Frances Welford, in pursuance of power contained in said will of said Basil Welford, did nominate and appoint said Richard Clare to be a trustee for all purposes of said will of said Basil Welford in place of said Robert Spearton, and to act in conjunction with said Raymond Welford.

Executed by all parties and attested.

1870,
May 17th.
Said Charles Welford died an infant aged 9 years.

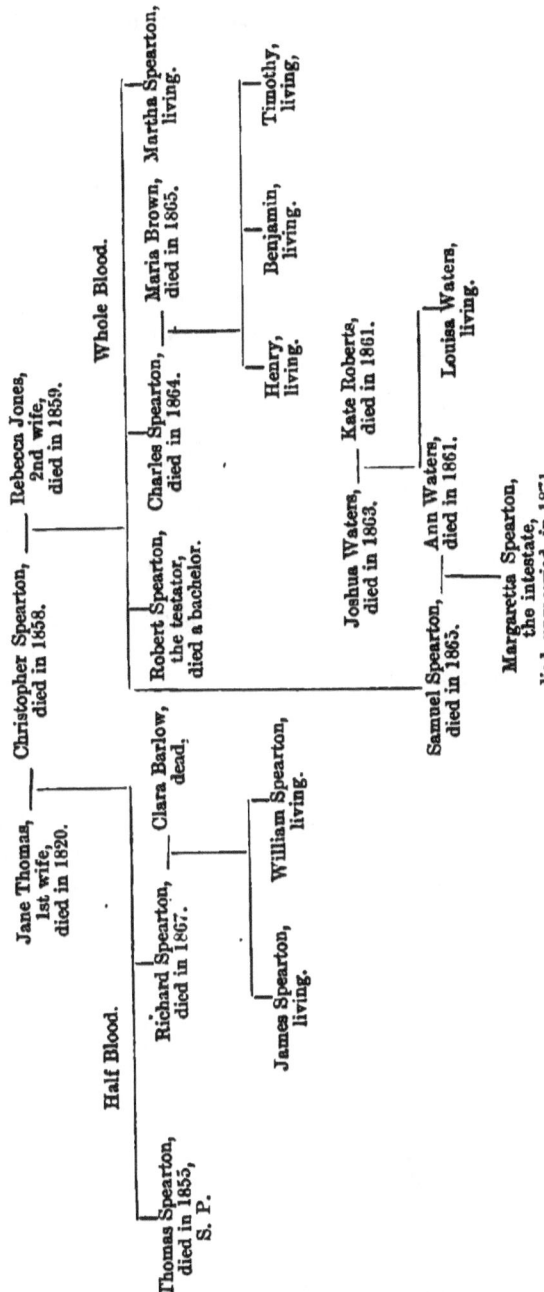

1871,
July 3rd.

Said Margaretta Spearton died an infant of the age of 13 years and unmarried.

Said Frances Welford (the widow of said Basil Welford) is living.

As to the 40 Shares in the L—— and W—— Bank.

These 40 shares were purchased in the joint names of the testator, Robert Spearton, and of Raymond Welford, and at the death of said Robert Spearton the 40 shares were standing in their joint names, as the registered proprietors, in the bank books.

The 40 shares, in fact, were originally the sole absolute property of the said Basil Welford at the time of his death. Robert Spearton and Raymond Welford held the shares in trust for Basil Welford, and he received the bank dividends up to the time of his death.

On the death of said Robert Spearton notice of the above facts was given by his executors to the bank, and that said Raymond Welford was a trustee of said shares for the executors of said Basil Welford and Robert Spearton, and application was made to the bank for payment of the dividends on the shares to said Raymond Welford as the surviving proprietor.

The bank declined to pay the dividends to said Raymond Welford, and required that a transfer of the shares should be made by the executors of Robert Spearton and Raymond Welford to said Raymond Welford, so as to make him the sole registered proprietor before payment of the dividends to him.

The following letter was received by Mr. Spearton's executors from the solicitors of the bank, dated 19th December, 1869 :—

"L—— and W—— Bank. 40 shares standing in joint names of Robert Spearton and Raymond Welford. .

"We have received your letter and the form of memorandum which you propose should be signed by the executors of Mr. Robert Spearton.

" The scope of the Bank Deed of Constitution is to prevent any person from becoming the owner of shares in the bank without also taking upon himself the duties and responsibilities of a registered proprietor in respect of such shares.

" For this purpose the directors have power to require executors, &c., claiming shares by devolution in right of a registered proprietor, to execute the Deed of Constitution, and thereby become members of the co-partnership, under penalty of the forfeiture of the shares for the general benefit of the Company.

" Therefore, it is necessary for the executors either to become members in respect of these shares jointly with Mr. Raymond Welford, or to allow them to devolve into his sole name, when they would be at his absolute disposal, as the Deed of Constitution protects the bank from all notice or liability in respect of trusts of shares, and only acknowledges the registered proprietor as absolute owner. To this course (as we understand) your clients have no objection, from the confidence they have in Mr. Raymond Welford.

" We have therefore altered your form for the purpose of putting on record the fact of your clients the executors declining to become members of the Company in respect of these shares, and, upon your returning it to us signed by the executors of Mr. Robert Spearton, the bank will enter the shares in the sole name of Mr. Raymond Welford.

" Where parties disclaim (which the executors in this case object to do) on account of their having (as executors) a beneficial contingent interest in the shares, it is the practice to put that disclaimer on record in the form of a transfer; and we still think the form of a transfer the most convenient. The beneficial interest is distinct from the legal interest, and remains bound in the hands of the surviving joint holder, and there will be no occasion for any disclaimer of the beneficial interest in joining in the transfer."

Form of notice to Bank that the executors declined to become members of the Bank Company:—

" Whereas Robert Spearton, of No.   ,   , in the county of   , died on the 19th day of

September, 1860, having duly made his will, dated the 27th day of August, 1868, and thereof appointed the undersigned, and   , executors. And the said will was proved by the said   in the principal registry of Her Majesty's Court of Probate on the 23rd day of October, 1869. And the probate thereof has been duly registered in the books of the   Bank in respect of 40 shares in the said bank, which at the time of the decease of the said testator stood in the register books of the said bank in the joint names of the said testator Robert Spearton and Raymond Welford, who is still living. Now, therefore, we the said   (as such executors as aforesaid) do hereby give you notice that we decline to become members of the bank in respect of the said 40 shares.

"Dated this   day of   , 1870.

"Signed   (by Executors).

"To the Directors and Manager of the   Bank."

As to Railway Debentures.

Declaration of death and identity.

I, A—— B——, of   , in the county of   , gentleman, solemnly and sincerely declare that I knew and was well acquainted with Robert Spearton, late of   , in the county of   , the person named in the Register of   , of the   Railway Company, as the owner, jointly with Raymond Welford, of   , of the following debenture bonds of the said Company, namely, No.   , dated 18   , &c. [set out numbers and dates]. And I further solemnly and sincerely declare that the said Robert Spearton died on the 19th day of September, 1869, and is the same person as is mentioned and referred to in the certificate of death hereunto annexed.

A certificate of death to be obtained.

And I make, &c,

ABSTRACT No. 18.   99

TRANSFER OF EAST INDIAN RAILWAY DEBENTURES TO
TRUSTEES.

I, Raymond Welford, of   , the survivor in a joint account with Robert Spearton, deceased, in consideration of the sum of five shillings paid to me by Richard Clare, of   , do hereby transfer to the said Raymond Welford and Richard Clare, their executors, administrators, and assigns,   debentures, No.   [set out numbers], series   , dated   18   , made by the   Railway Company to the said Robert Spearton and Raymond Welford for securing the principal sums of £   and interest, and also the said   several principal sums of £   and all interest due and to grow due thereon respectively, and all my right, title, estate, benefit, and interest in respect of the said securities and in and to the monies thereby respectively secured. In witness whereof I have hereunto set my hand and seal this   day of   , 1870.

Signed, sealed, and delivered by the }
  above-named Raymond Welford,   }
  in the presence of   }

TRANSFER OF RAILWAY MORTGAGE BONDS TO TRUSTEES in a case where one trustee is dead and another trustee retires from the trust, and two new trustees are appointed in the place of the deceased and retiring trustees.

We, A——, of   , B——, of   , and C——, of   , the survivors in a joint account with D——, deceased, in consideration of the sum of five shillings paid to us by the said B—— and C—— and E——, of   , and F——, of   , do hereby transfer to the said B——, C——, E——, and F——, their executors, administrators, and assigns,   mortgage bonds, No.   , and No.   , made by the   Railway Company to the said   , bearing date the   day of   , 18   , for securing several sums of   pounds and   pounds and interest, and all our right, estate, and interest in and to

H 2

the money and interest thereby secured, and in and to the undertaking, rates, tolls, sums of money, and property thereby respectively assigned, as witness our hands and seals this   day of   , 1870.

Signed, sealed, and delivered by the above-named   , in the presence of

---

No. 19.

COPYHOLD.—Equitable estate tail barred. Power to executors to sell.

Abstract of the Title of Mr. Robert Jason and another, as trustees and executors of the will of Mr. James Hadley, to two Copyhold messuages and twenty-four acres of customary land, situate at   , in the parish of A——, in the county of B——, held of the manor of D——.

Manor of D——, in the county of B——.

1812, September 7th. At a Court held this day, the Homage, upon their oaths, presented the death of Richard Phillips, late a customary tenant of the manor, and that he, by Roll of Court held the 23rd of October, 1802, was seized to him and his heirs of

Two copyhold or customary messuages or tenements, with their appurtenances, and six closes or parcels of customary land adjoining thereto, containing altogether, by estimation, twenty-four acres, situate, lying, and being near the Hall of A——, in the parish of A——, within the said manor, formerly the estate of John Brooks, Esq., and held of the said manor by the annual rent of four shillings.

And that Christopher Phillips, of   , gentleman, was the only brother and customary heir of said Richard

Phillips, deceased; whereupon said Christopher Phillips appeared in person and craved to be admitted tenant of said hereditaments. And the lord, by his steward, granted and delivered seizin to him by the rod of same premises.

> To hold same premises unto said Christopher Phillips, his heirs and assigns, for ever, at the will of the lord, according to custom, &c.

Surrender by said Christopher Phillips and Martha, his wife, of
    All said premises.
    And reversion, &c., and all estate, &c.
To use of Jonathan Parker, of   , and his heirs and assigns for ever.
Upon condition that if said Christopher Phillips, his heirs, executors, administrators, or assigns, should pay to said Jonathan Parker, his executors, administrators, or assigns, the sum of £500, with lawful interest for same, on or before the 27th May, 1835, the said surrender to be void, or else to remain in full force and virtue.

1834,
May 27th.

Presentment by Homage of an instrument, endorsed upon last abstracted conditional surrender, authorising steward of said manor to enter satisfaction acknowledged upon court rolls of same manor of said principal sum of £500, and all interest, which instrument was under the hand of Mary Parker (therein described as the daughter and executrix of will of said Jonathan Parker), and dated 8th January, 1842.

1842,
January 9th.

Presentment of surrender, dated 6th October, 1850, by said Christopher Phillips, of
    All his copyhold or customary messuages, lands, and hereditaments, held of said manor,
To use of his will.

1850,
November 4th.

Probate copy will of said Christoper Phillips, whereby (*inter alia*) said testator gave and devised
    All his copyhold messuages, lands, and property, held of said. manor of D——, in said county of B——, unto and to use of his friend, Benjamin Travis, of   , his heirs and assigns, for ever, upon following trusts (that is to say) :—

1853,
March 14th.

ABSTRACT No. 19.

In trust for Martha Phillips (the wife of said testator) and her assigns during her life . . . . remainder.
In trust for the testator's three children, Peter Phillips, Charles Phillips, and Ada Phillips, and the heirs of their respective bodies lawfully issuing, with cross remainders between or among them . . remainder.
In trust for Edward Phillips (the brother of said testator) and the heirs of his body lawfully issuing. . .
. . . . . . remainder.
In trust for testator's right heirs.

Signed by said Christopher Phillips, and attested by two witnesses.

1856,
February 4th.
Said Christopher Phillips died.

1856,
April 23rd.
Said will proved by said Martha Phillips (the executrix) in Consistory Court of Bishop of L——.

1857,
June 19th.
Said Ada Phillips died an infant, aged nineteen, and unmarried.

1856,
July 1st.
Admission of said Benjamin Travis.
At a Court held this day, the Homage presented that at a General Court, held 23rd April, 1856, the Homage presented that said Christopher Phillips, late a customary tenant of said manor, who, whilst he lived, held by copy of court roll by the yearly rent of 4s.
All, &c. [parcels, as in admission of 1812.]
To which he was admitted at a Court held 7th September, 1812, had, since the last Court, died thereof seized. But who was entitled to said premises the Homage knew not.

Whereupon, at that and the following Court, proclamations were made for the customary heir of said Christopher Phillips, or other person or persons entitled to said premises, to come into Court and be admitted tenant or tenants thereof, or else the same would be seized into the hands of the lord of the manor for want of a tenant; but no one came.

Presentment by the Homage of the will of said testator, Christopher Phillips, dated 14th March, 1853, whereby he gave and devised to said Benjamin Travis and his heirs,

All his (testator's) customary estates, held of said
   manor,
To hold to said Benjamin Travis and his heirs upon
certain trusts in said will expressed.

Which said will was duly proved in Consistory Court
of the Bishop of L——, on the 23rd day of April, 1856.

And the said Benjamin Travis having appeared and
craved admission and seizin of said premises, the same
was granted and delivered to him by the lord of said
manor, by the hands of the steward, by the rod.

To hold said copyhold premises, with appurtenances,
to said Benjamin Travis, his heirs and assigns, for ever,
pursuant to and upon the trusts thereof declared by said
will of said Christopher Phillips.

At the will, &c., according to the custom, &c., at a
quit rent of 4s.

And by suit and service.

Signed by steward.

Said Charles Phillips died an infant, aged fifteen years, and unmarried.   1858, October 19th.

DISENTAIL.

Indenture of this date made between said Peter Phillips, of first part, said Martha Phillips (widow), of second part, and James Brand, of   , of third part,   1858, November 23rd.

> Reciting said abstracted admission of 7th September, 1812.
>
> And reciting said will of said Christopher Phillips, and his death and proof of will.
>
> And reciting said abstracted admission of 1st July, 1856.
>
> And reciting deaths of said Ada Phillips and Charles Phillips, both intestate, infants and unmarried.
>
> And reciting that said Peter Phillips, with the consent and concurrence of said Martha Phillips (as protector of the settlement created by said recited will of said Christopher Phillips), was desirous of barring his equitable estate tail, created by said will, in the said copyhold hereditaments, and all reversions and remainders expectant or dependent thereupon, and all estates, rights, powers, and interests, to take effect after the determination or in defeasance thereof, and to acquire the fee of said copyhold premises, according to custom

of said manor (subject to life interest of said Martha Phillips therein).

It is by abstracting indenture witnessed that, for effectuating said desire, said Peter Phillips, with the consent and concurrence of said Martha Phillips (testified by her execution of abstracting indenture), did grant and convey to said John Brand and his heirs—

> All and singular said copyhold or customary messuages, closes, pieces or parcels of land, and hereditaments, devised by said will of said Christopher Phillips, and to which he was admitted tenant at the said Court, held on the said 7th day of September, 1812, as aforesaid, with the appurtenances,
> And all estate, &c.

To hold same premises (subject and without prejudice to life estate of said Martha Phillips therein) unto said John Brand and his heirs,

To use of said Peter Phillips, his heirs and assigns, for ever, to be held by copy of court roll, according to custom of said manor (freed and discharged from said equitable estate tail in remainder of said Peter Phillips, and from all reversions and remainders, expectant or dependent thereupon, and all estates, rights, interests, and powers to take effect after the determination or in defeasance of such estate tail).

Executed by all said parties, and attested.

1869, March 27th. Said Martha Phillips died.

1869, August 15th. Admission of James Hadley, of , upon the surrender of said Benjamin Travis and Peter Phillips, and Elizabeth, his wife (she being examined apart, &c.), in consideration of £2,400, as tenant to

> All those, the said copyhold or customary messuages and lands, hereinbefore described, formerly the estate of Richard Phillips (by similar description as before), to all which premises said Benjamin Travis was admitted tenant at said Court held on 1st July, 1856.

ABSTRACT No. 19.

To hold said premises, with the appurtenances, unto said James Hadley, his heirs and assigns, for ever, according to custom of said manor, at rent, &c.

Signed by steward.

Probate copy will of said James Hadley, whereby, after directing payment of his just debts and funeral and testamentary expenses by his executors, thereinafter named, he appointed Robert Jason, of   , and Samuel Ring, executors and trustees of his will.

1870,
November 27th.

Said testator authorised and empowered the said Robert Jason and Samuel Ring, or the survivor of them, or the executors or administrators of such survivor, as soon as conveniently might be after testator's death, to sell and dispose of all his copyhold or customary estates and hereditaments, situate in and held of the manor of D——, in the county of B——, either together or in lots, and either by public auction or private contract, and subject to such restrictive conditions as they or he should think proper. And the said testator willed that the nett moneys to be raised by sale of the said premises should be taken as part of and go along with the residue of his personal estate, according as the same was thereinafter disposed of.

And the said testator willed that the receipt or receipts, in writing, of said Robert Jason and Samuel Ring, or the survivor of them, or the executors or administrators of such survivor, should from time to time be a sufficient discharge to the purchaser or purchasers of said copyhold premises, who should not be answerable for or chargeable with any non-application or misapplication of such moneys, or any part thereof, or be concerned to make any inquiry as to the propriety of such sale or sales.

Signed by said James Hadley,
and attested by two witnesses.

Said James Hadley died.

1872,
April 17th.

Will of said James Hadley proved by said Robert

1872,
May 3rd.

Jason and Samuel Ring in Her Majesty's Court of Probate, at Principal Registry.

The trustees and executors of the will of Mr. James Hadley have agreed to sell the copyhold estate, comprised in admission of 1812, to Mr. N——.

No. 20.

LEASEHOLDS FOR YEARS.—Abstract of the Title of Arthur Thomas Dornton, Esquire, to four Leasehold messuages, situate and being Nos. 5, 6, 7, and 8 in R—— Square, in the parish of St.   , in the county of Middlesex.

1840,   By indenture of lease of this date, made between
September 29th Charles Thompson, of, &c., builder, of the one part, and Heinrich von Kohn,   , of, &c., of the other part,

It is witnessed that in consideration of the expense, costs, and charges, which he the said Heinrich von Kohn had been at in erecting the messuages or tenements, erections and buildings, thereinafter described; and also for and in consideration of the yearly rent thereinafter contained, and on the part and behalf of the said Heinrich von Kohn,   his executors, administrators, and assigns, to be paid, kept, done, and performed, he the said Charles Thompson did demise and lease unto the said Henrich von Kohn,   his executors, administrators, and assigns, all that piece or· parcel of ground situate, lying, and being in a new square intended to be called R—— Square, in the parish of St.   , in the county of Middlesex, fronting towards the north upon   , and towards the west upon other ground intended to be demised to   , and

ABSTRACT No. 20. 107

abutting and adjoining towards the south upon
a messuage or tenement and ground demised to
         , and towards the east upon ground in-
tended to be demised to   , and containing
from north to south, as well on the east front as
on the west front or rear thereof, 300 feet, little
more or less, and from west to east, as well on
the north as on the south side thereof, including
the forecourts and gardens, 200 feet, little more
or less, which piece or parcel of ground, intended
to be demised by the now abstracting indenture
of lease, was more particularly delineated and
described in the plan or ground plot thereof,
drawn in the margin of the now abstracting
indenture, and was thereon coloured pink;

Together with the four messuages or tenements
erected and built on the said piece or parcel of
ground or upon some part thereof; and all other
erections and buildings then erecting or to be
erected and built upon the said piece of ground
thereby demised, or upon any part thereof.

And all ways, &c.

To hold the same premises to said Heinich von
Kohn from the 25th day of March, 1840, for 98 years
and one-half of another year, wanting 21 days.

At the yearly rent of £40, payable quarterly.

Covenants by said Heinrich von Kohn:
 To pay said yearly rent.
 To pay land tax, and all other rates and taxes.
 To repair.
 To deliver up premises at end of term, with all
  fixtures.
 To pay proportion for repairing party walls and
  sewers, &c.
 Not to carry on trade or business of, &c. [set out
  restricted trades], without the licence and consent in writing of said Charles Thompson, his
  executors, administrators, or assigns.
 To permit said Charles Thompson and the superior
  landlord or landlords, &c., to enter and view state
  of repair, and to repair on notice.
 To insure in full value of premises, and to lay out
  insurance money in rebuilding premises.

ABSTRACT No. 20.

N.B.—The lease abstracted appears to be an under lease, and the property (with other property) appears to be subject to a superior rent, &c., and to the lessee's covenants in the original lease.

Covenants by said Charles Thompson:
For quiet enjoyment by lessee.
And to indemnify said Heinrich von Kohn from the payment of the rents and performance of clauses and agreements reserved and contained by and in the original indenture of lease dated the 25th day of March, 1840, made between, &c., under which the said Charles Thompson then held the said ground and premises, with other ground and messuages; and to produce the said original lease.

Executed by said Charles Thompson, and attested.

1840,
September 30th

Registered in Middlesex, B.   , No.   .

1862,
September 24th

By indenture of this date made between said Heinrich von Kohn, of the one part, and Richard Thomas Dornton, of   , in the county of   , Esquire, of the other part,
After reciting the before abstracted indenture of lease, and reciting that said R. T. Dornton had contracted and agreed with said Heinrich von Kohn for the absolute purchase of the said four messuages and ground comprised in said lease for the residue of said term for the sum of £2,000,

It is witnessed that in consideration of £2,000 paid by said R. T. Dornton to said Heinrich von Kohn at or before the execution, &c., the receipt, &c., said Heinrich von Kohn did grant, assign, and confirm unto said Richard Thomas Dornton, his executors, administrators, and assigns,

The said piece of ground, four messuages or tenements, and premises comprised in and demised by said abstracted indenture of lease of the 29th day of September, 1840, which four messuages were then in the occupations of A, B, C, and D, and were known as Nos. 5, 6, 7, and 8, in R——Square aforesaid.
With the fixtures and appurtenances.

To hold the same premises unto said R. T. Dornton,

his executors, administrators, and assigns, thenceforth during all the residue then to come of the said term of 98 years and one-half of another year (wanting 21 days) created by said abstracted indenture of lease,

> Subject (as from the date of abstracting indenture) to the payment of the rent and performance of the covenants reserved and contained by and in said abstracted lease.

Covenants by said Heinrich von Kohn:
That said lease was good and subsisting.
That the rent and covenants had been paid and performed.
That he had good right to assign.
For quiet enjoyment.
Free from incumbrances; and
For further assurance.

Covenant by said R. T. Dornton for payment of rent and performance of covenants.

Executed by both parties and attested.

Receipt for £2,000 endorsed, signed by Von Kohn, and witnessed.

Registered in Middlesex, 10th October, 1862, B. , No. .

1868, May 4th.

Probate copy will of said Richard Thomas Dornton, whereby (*inter alia*) said testator gave and bequeathed to his daughter Maria Dornton an annuity of £100 during her life, to be paid quarterly.

And testator charged all his freehold and leasehold estates with the payment of said annuity.

And (subject to the payment of said annuity and to the payment of testator's debts and funeral and testamentary expenses) said testator gave, devised, and bequeathed—

> All his freehold and leasehold messuages, lands, and estates,

unto his son, Arthur Thomas Dornton, his heirs, executors, and administrators absolutely.

And testator appointed said Arthur Thomas Dornton sole executor of his said will.

> Signed by said testator in presence of two witnesses, and attested.

1870, Said Richard Thomas Dornton died.
November 14th.

1871, Said will proved by said Arthur Thomas Dornton at
March 4th. Principal Registry of Her Majesty's Court of Probate.

1872, By indenture of mortgage made between said Arthur
October 19th. Thomas Dornton (thereinafter called the mortgagor) of one part, and Charles Radford and Christopher Hensley (trustees of the   Permanent Benefit Building Society, thereinafter called the mortgagees), of the other part,

> After reciting said first abstracted indenture of lease, and that the mortgagor was possessed of the premises during the residue of the said term, and reciting that the mortgagor, being a member of the said society, had subscribed for   shares in the said society, and had applied to the directors to advance him £400, which they had agreed to do, to be repaid by the monthly instalments of £   during the period of   years, from   day of   , 1878, with interest in the meantime from the date of abstracting indenture up to said   day of   , 1878,

It was witnessed that in consideration of £400 to said mortgagor paid by said directors, the receipt, &c., the said mortgagor did demise unto said mortgagees
> The said piece of ground, four messuages or tenements, and premises comprised in and demised by said abstracted indenture of lease of 29th September, 1840, with the appurtenances.

To hold same premises, together with all fixtures, unto said mortgagees for the residue of said term by said lease granted (except the last ten days thereof),
> Upon trust to permit said mortgagor to receive the rents thereof so long as he should pay said interest and subscriptions.

Usual power to demise and sell in case of default.

ABSTRACT No. 20.

Covenant by said mortgagor to pay said interest and subscriptions, and in the event of paying off said principal sum on or before said   day of   , 1878, to pay an additional sum of £

Covenant by said mortgagor to pay said monthly instalments after said   day of   , 1878.
To perform lessee's covenants in said lease.
That he had good right to demise.
For quiet enjoyment after default.
For further assurance.

    Executed by said Arthur Thomas Dornton, and attested.

    Receipt for £500 endorsed, signed by Dornton, and witnessed.

Registered in Middlesex, 23rd October, 1872, B.   ,   No.   .

Copy receipt endorsed on last abstracted mortgage.

We, the undersigned, the Trustees for the time being of the within-mentioned   Permanent Benefit Building Society, do hereby acknowledge to have received of and from the within-named Arthur Thomas Dornton, his executors, administrators, or assigns, all monies intended to be ecured by the within-written deed.

As witness our hands, this 4th day of March, 1873.

 Witness,   Charles Radford.
 A―― B――.   Christopher Hensley.

PART II.

OBSERVATIONS, REQUISITIONS, &c., ON THE FOREGOING ABSTRACTS.

No. 1.—Abstract.

FREEHOLD TITLE.

GARFORD'S TITLE.

Observations on Title.

Some satisfactory evidence must be furnished that Percival Garford was seized in fee simple of the estate at the date of his will in 1820, and how he became seized; and, in fact, a title must be shown for 60 years. And it must be shown that from the time of the death of Percival Garford his daughter Maria had peaceable possession or received the rents of the estate up to her death. Have any leases (or agreements with tenants) been granted of the property? if so, they should be abstracted and produced.

On the death of Percival Garford in 1826, his daughter Maria became tenant in tail in possession of the estate in question.

It is stated in the abstract—

That Maria Garford married Robert Charlton, and that the only issue of this marriage was a son, Joseph Charlton, who died in 1844, an infant.

That Selina Garford married Charles Turner, and died in 1858, without having had issue, and that Charles Turner is living.

That Maria Charlton died in 1864, without leaving any issue, and that Robert Charlton is living.

On the death of Maria Charlton, her husband, Robert Charlton, became entitled to the estate during his life as tenant by the curtesy of England.

Charles Turner has no interest in the estate, his wife never having been in possession.

A careful search must be made at the Public Record Office, from the death of Percival Garford, for fines and recoveries by Maria Garford and Selina Garford (both before and since their marriages), and since 1833 for deeds of disentail by them, and it must be ascertained that neither of them barred her estate tail. Search should also be made at the Common Pleas Office in Lancaster Place, for deeds, acknowledged by either of them under the Fines and Recoveries Act; and search should also be made at the Public Record Office and at the Chancery Inrolment Office for deeds of disentail by Peter Garford and Robert Thomas Garford.

Assuming that it will be clearly ascertained that neither of the daughters of the testator, or either of the present vendors, have barred their estates tail, and the remainders over, the effect of the limitations in the will to Peter Garford and Robert Thomas Garford will require to be considered.

This limitation (in default of issue of the testator's daughters) is, as to one moiety of the estate, to Peter Garford and his heirs, and if he dies without issue, over; this limitation (on the authority of various cases), created an estate tail in Peter Garford. Under the limitation to Peter Garford and his heirs, his issue may be included, and there is nothing in the construction of an estate tail repugnant to the language of the testator— the word "heirs" being supposed to be used in the restricted sense of "heirs of the body." As to the other moiety, this being devised to Robert Thomas Garford for his life, and if he dies without issue, over, will also create an estate tail in Robert Thomas Garford. See Lee's Case, 1 Leon. 285; and various modern cases. In this case there being no express gift to any class of issue, an estate tail is therefore implied in Robert Thomas Garford, in which (there being no intermediate remainders) his life estate immediately merges.

Peter Garford and Robert Thomas Garford must execute disentailing assurances of their moieties of the estate. Robert Charlton (as protector of the settlement created by the will) must concur in these assurances to consent, and to convey his life interest as tenant by the curtesy. These assurances must be enrolled in Chancery within six months; or the disentail may be effected in the conveyance to the purchaser; in which case the vendors should pay the expense of immediate enrolment.

A statutory declaration by some disinterested person well acquainted with the family as to the following facts, and identifying the parties, should be furnished (with certificates), viz. :—
    Death or burial of Percival Garford.
    Marriage and death of Maria Charlton.
    Birth or baptism and death of Joseph Charlton.
    Marriage and death of Selina Turner.
    Death of Catherine Garford.

And the several places and dates of the marriages, birth or baptism, and deaths or burials of the parties respectively should be stated.

That Maria Charlton and Selina Turner both died without having barred their estates tail.

That Maria Charlton had no other child than Joseph Charlton, and was only married once; and that Selina Turner died without having had any issue, and was only married once.

The certificates necessary to verify the above declaration should be produced and made exhibits thereto.

Receipts must be produced showing the payment of the annuity of £300 to Catherine Garford; and also a receipt from her personal representative for a proportionate part of the annuity up to the date of her death; and probate of her will, or letters of administration of her personal estate, should be produced; and the receipt for the succession duty which became payable on the death of Catherine Garford on the cesser of the annuity of £300 must be produced, and handed to the purchaser.

Application must be made to the Commissioners of Inland Revenue under the 41st section of the Succession Duty Act (16 and 17 Vic. c. 51) to commute and receive the succession duty presumptively to be paid by the vendors on the death of Robert Charlton. The duty must be paid by the vendors, and the receipt must be handed to the purchaser.

The 18th section of the act appears to exempt Robert Charlton from succession duty, by reference to the Legacy Duty Acts.

See General Observations and Requisitions from No. 5 to the conclusion of the General Observations and Requisitions. All these must be considered and attended to, so far as they are applicable to this title.

No. 2.—ABSTRACT.

FREEHOLD.

GOODWIN'S TITLE.

Requisitions and Observations.

1. Was Robert Charles Corbet married at the date of the indenture of 15th July, 1810 ? If so, is his wife or widow now living ?
See General Observation, No. 2.

2. Is John Thorburn, the trustee in the indenture of 2nd January, 1828, now living ? If so, he must join in the conveyance to the purchaser, and convey according to his interest ; or his death must be shown.

3. Had Christopher Limond a wife at the date of indenture of 23rd June, 1864, who was married to him before 1834 ? If so, she must release her right to dower.
See General Observation, No. 2.

4. Under the will of Robert Limond the legal estate in fee simple was devised to Charles Porter and Abraham Walton upon trust; these trustees, or the survivor (if living), or his heir or devisee, must concur in the conveyance to the purchaser.
See General Observation, No. 1.

5. The mortgage debt of £2,000 secured by the mortgage of 20th February, 1870, must be paid off out of the purchase-money; and the surviving mortgagee must join in the conveyance. There is no declaration in the mortgage that the mortgagees were to be entitled to the mortgage debt and interest as joint tenants. There is no survivorship in equity between mortgagees. The will of Thomas Bryan must be abstracted, and the probate or letters of administration of his effects must be produced ; and his executors or administrators must concur in the conveyance to admit that they have no interest in the mortgage debt.

6. Some evidence must be furnished showing that the descriptions of the property in the abstract include the lands comprised in the particular of sale and contract ; this can be done by furnishing tracings from the tithe commutation map of the parish, and the old leases, &c.,

and by a statutory declaration by some person acquainted with the property.

7. How is the property purchased now held by the tenants? Are there any leases or agreements with the tenants? If so, they should be produced and abstracted.

8. What are the outgoings payable in respect of the property sold?

9. What documents will be handed to the purchaser?

10. A statutory declaration by some disinterested person well acquainted as to the following facts, and identifying the parties, should be furnished (with certificates), viz. :—

> Death or burial of Arthur Vallotton.
> Death or burial of Clara Vallotton, and evidence that she died without issue, an infant, and unmarried.
> Death of John Thorburn, the trustee, if dead.
> Death of Thomas Bryan.
> Death of Robert Limond.
> Death of Christopher Limond, and evidence that he died unmarried and without issue, or that his issue has failed; this evidence is most important.

And the several places and dates of the deaths or burials of the parties should be stated.

The certificates necessary to verify the above declaration should be produced and made exhibits thereto.

11. Are there any rights of way or other easements over or affecting the estate? If so, state them. Is there any claim for compensation by the tenant for acts of husbandry done by him on the farm?

12. Have any of the persons named in the abstract (to the knowledge of the vendor or his solicitor) been bankrupt, or taken the benefit of any of the Insolvent Debtors' Acts? If so, when?

13. Has any money been borrowed under the Drainage or Land Improvement Acts, and charged upon the estate?

14. Are there any judgments, pendentes lites, annuities, incumbrances, deeds or facts, relating to the property sold to the purchaser within the knowledge of the vendor or his solicitor, which are not disclosed by the abstract? If so, state the same.

No. 3.—ABSTRACT.

COPYHOLD TITLE.

PENISTAN'S TITLE.

Purchaser's Requisitions.	*Vendor's Replies.*
1. It appears that a heriot is payable on the death of a tenant? Is it payable on any other occasion? This is the case in some manors.	
2. The will of Jacob Penistan would appear to have been unattested. How it is shown that the copyhold estate was well devised by this will?	Previously to the passing of the Wills Act, 1 Vic., c. 26 (Act E), copyhold estates would pass by an unattested will; the will of Jacob Penistan was made in 1830. The Wills Act does not apply to a will made before 1st Jan., 1838, although the testator died after that date; therefore this will was sufficient to pass this copyhold estate.
3. It must be clearly shown that Maria Penistan survived her mother, otherwise the estate would appear beneficially to belong to the children of the testator's son, Robert Penistan.	There will be no difficulty in showing that Maria Penistan survived her mother.
4. It is stated that by the custom of the manor the descent is to the youngest son or youngest brother. The certificate of the steward of the manor as to this custom must be procured.	
5. It is stated that Maria Penistan died intestate; this must be shown by the production of letters of adminis-	

| *Purchaser's Requisitions.* | *Vendor's Replies.* |

tration to her personal estate, and by a statutory declaration by the solicitor of the family, or by some other mode, as to the fact of the intestacy of Maria Penistan.

6. Evidence that George Penistan is the youngest brother (of the whole blood) of Maria Penistan must be furnished. To prove this, a certificate of the marriage of Jacob Penistan must be furnished, and also certificates of the births or baptisms of George Penistan, and the other sons of Jacob Penistan; and a pedigree of the Penistan family, and a statutory declaration by some person acquainted with the family, that George Penistan is the youngest brother (of the whole blood) of Maria Penistan. George Penistan must be admitted tenant on the court roll.

7. What documents of title will be handed to the purchaser? If the deed of 27th October, 1860, is not handed to the purchaser, he must have an attested copy of it, and a covenant for its production.

8. What stamp is on the mortgage of 27th October, 1860?

9. The mortgagee must be paid off, and satisfaction of the conditional surrender of 17th June, 1870, must be entered on the court rolls.

                                          This will be done on the completion of the purchase.

Purchaser's Requisitions. *Vendor's Replies.*

10. The court rolls of the manor must be carefully searched, to ascertain that the abstract is correct and complete.

11. Has any charge been made on the estate under the Drainage and Land Improvement Acts?

Search should be made for any such charges, at the office of the Inclosure Commissioners, No. 3, St. James's Square.

12. Are there any rights of road or way over the estate, or any other easement affecting the property? If so, state the particulars.

13. Is the vendor, or is his solicitor aware of any surrender, charge, lien, judgment, lis pendens, annuity, writ of execution, or any other deed or incumbrance affecting the property which is not disclosed by the abstract?

14. Search should be made for judgments, lis pendens, writs of execution and annuities, as against Maria Penistan and George Penistan, and also in bankruptcy and insolvency, and for deeds of composition with creditors.

15. The receipt for the succession duty, which became payable on the death of Maria Penistan, must be produced and handed to the purchaser on completion.

Purchaser's Requisitions.	Vendor's Replies.
16. Is the estate or any part of it under lease or agreement for lease? If so, the leases or agreement should be abstracted and produced. Inquiry should be made of the tenants, and also whether any of them claim compensation for acts of husbandry. The counterparts of leases and agreements should be handed to the purchaser on completion.	
17. Certificates of the deaths of Judith Penistan and Maria Penistan to be produced, and evidence of their identity, by statutory declaration.	
18. See observation (17) on Denton's Title (Abstract No. 9), as to covenants for title.	

No. 4.—ABSTRACT.

LEASEHOLD FOR YEARS.

SETON'S TITLE.

Requisitions of Purchaser's Solicitor.	Replies of Vendor's Solicitor.
1. The receipts for the ground rent and taxes and outgoings up to the day fixed for completion of the pur-	

Requisitions of Purchaser's Solicitor.	*Replies of Vendor's Solicitor.*
chase, must be produced to the purchaser's solicitor.	
2. To what amount, and in whose names, and in what insurance office, has the property been insured against fire? The policy of insurance and the receipts for the premiums must be produced to the purchaser's solicitor; and the policy of insurance should be transferred to the purchaser.	
3. Have the succession duties which became payable on the respective deaths of Samuel Allen, Walter Jones, and Charles Seton in respect of the property sold, been paid? If not, they should be paid before the completion of the purchase; and the receipts must be produced, and handed to the purchaser on completion.	3. In these cases, succession duties are not payable; the sales are made by the administrators; after payment of the debts of the intestates, and the expenses of the administration of the estates, the surplus of the estates may become liable to succession duty. It appears on the abstract that a mortgage debt of £1,000 is payable out of the estate of Charles Seton; the succession duty is not a charge on the property under the circumstances.
4. Have the several letters of administration been registered in Middlesex?	4. The Registrar of Deeds, &c., for Middlesex, will refuse to register the letters of administration. The registry acts only apply to those deeds, documents and incumbrances which are executed or created by the acts of the parties interested. The

Requisitions of Purchaser's Solicitor.	*Replies of Vendor's Solicitor.*
	letters of administration are acts of the Court of Probate, and cannot be registered.

5. Is the vendor, or is her solicitor, aware of any breach or breaches of any of the lessee's covenants contained in the lease?

If so, state the particulars.

6. Have any or either, and which of the persons mentioned in the abstract, to the knowledge of the vendor or her solicitor, been declared bankrupt, or become insolvent debtors under any of the Insolvent Acts? And if so, which of the parties, and when? State the particulars.

7. The identity of the property with that described in the lease of 3rd April, 1850, must be shown.

8. Do the tenants of either of the houses hold under any leases or agreements for leases? If so, an abstract of the leases or agreements must be furnished, and the originals must be produced for examination. What notice must be given to determine the tenancies?

9. The mortgage debt must be paid off, and the mortgagee must concur in the assignment to the purchaser, at the vendor's expense.

This will be done.

10. When and where was

10. The conditions of

Requisitions of Purchaser's Solicitor.	Replies of Vendor's Solicitor.
Samuel Allen buried? A certificate of his death must be furnished.	sale stipulate that all certificates, &c., are to be searched for and obtained at the expense of the purchaser. It shall be ascertained where the several parties were buried.
11. The like question as to Walter Jones.	
12. The like as to Charles Seton.	
13. Is the vendor, or is her solicitor, aware of any settlement, mortgage, lien, charge, lease, judgment, crown debt, lis pendens, writ of execution, or other incumbrance or matter whatsoever, not disclosed by the abstract, which in any way affects the title to any part of the property sold, or the ability of the vendor to make a good title thereto?	The purchaser's solicitor can search the registry. [This requisition must be answered.]
14. The Registry of Deeds for Middlesex must be carefully searched, to ascertain if the abstract be correct and complete; and it must be ascertained that all the documents have been properly stamped.	
15. State the name and address of the person to whom the ground rent is payable.	

Requisitions of Purchaser's Solicitor.	Replies of Vendor's Solicitor.
16. The lease, letters of administration, and other documents abstracted, must be produced; and the purchaser reserves the right of making any further requisitions when these are answered, and the documents have been produced.	
To the vendor, and Mr.	, her solicitor.

Opinion of counsel as to payment of succession duty in respect of leaseholds, in cases where a sale is made by the personal representative of the deceased.

The duty payable in respect of leaseholds is clearly succession, and not legacy duty. See sections 1 and 19 of the Succession Duty Act, 1853. The succession duty, however, is made a charge not upon the very property itself, but upon the beneficial interest of the successor; and the personal representatives of the deceased have, for the purposes of administration, a paramount power to sell his leaseholds. If not so sold by them, then the leaseholds in the hands of the successor, or any person claiming under him, would be liable to the duty; but if so sold, then it appears to me that they would cease to be liable, and the duty be payable upon the portion of the sale monies coming to the successor. I do not think that a purchaser can, in the absence of special circumstances, be required to ascertain whether or not the sale is properly made by the personal representatives, as this would involve him in the administration of the estate of the deceased; and the fact of the personal representatives being also the legatees, or next of kin, of the deceased, does not, in my opinion, make any difference, provided the sale be made by them in their representative capacity.

I think, therefore, that the purchaser can safely complete the purchase of the leasehold in question without requiring evidence of the payment of the succession duty which became payable on the death of any of the parties (owners) who died intestate.

No. 5.—ABSTRACT.

FREEHOLD.

APPLETON'S TITLE.

Requisitions on behalf of Purchaser.	Replies of Vendor's Solicitor.
1. The title commences in 1832 (39 years since). A title must be deduced for 60 years, unless it has been stipulated that the earlier title shall not be required.	
2. Had Benjamin Stratton a wife living at the date of the mortgage of 9th January, 1832? If so, when did she die, and where was she buried? A certificate of her burial or death must be furnished, and evidence of her identity; or, if living, she must release her right to dower, unless barred of dower, which must be shown.	
3. The Master's Report of 29th April, 1849, and the order *nisi* of 4th May, 1849, should be abstracted in chief, and the abstract should be verified with the record, or with office copies of that report and order.	This Decree is a matter of record, and may be examined by the purchaser if he thinks proper so to do; the vendor has no other evidence of it than the recital.

Requisitions on behalf of Purchaser.	Replies of Vendor's Solicitor.
[Further requisition—the vendor is bound to comply with this requisition so far as it relates to an abstract in chief of the order of 4th May, 1849).]	[Office copy order obtained].
4. The abstract of the Decree of 10th June, 1840, in the suit "Combe v. Stratton," and of the Master's Report of 17th June, 1848, and of the order of 8th November, 1848, confirming that report, and of the order of 23rd May, 1849, confirming the sale to Jacob Appleton, should be verified with the record or with office copies of those proceedings.	The vendor has not office copies of these proceedings; they are all matters of record, and may be examined with the record at the purchaser's expense.
5. It is very questionable whether the gift in the will of Jacob Appleton of all his "Property," &c., passed the fee simple of his real estates to his nephew Richard Appleton. Who is the heir-at-law of Jacob Appleton? He should concur and join in the conveyance to the purchaser.	The word "Property" in a devise will pass the fee simple of real estates, unless from the context the gift appears to apply only to personal estate. Mr. Jarman (on Wills) cites numerous authorities to that effect. See the case of Lloyd v. Lloyd, 7, Law R. 458 (Equity Cases).
6. The receipt for the succession duty which became payable on the death of Jacob Appleton must be produced, and handed to the purchaser on completion.	This will be done.
7. An office copy of the decree of dissolution of the marriage between Thomas Gleppin and Mary Ann Ap-	

Requisitions on behalf of Purchaser.	Replies of Vendor's Solicitor.
pleton must be produced for examination with the abstract. How is it shown that the effect of the decree was to enable Mary Ann Appleton to dispose of property devised to her as if she were a *feme sole* and unmarried?	See the 25th section of 20 and 21 Vic., c. 85.
8. Richard Appleton by his will charged his real estates with the payment of his debts. Have the testator's debts been paid? This should be shown.	The testator's debts cannot be paid until his estates are sold. A devisee of real estates charged with debts had always power to sell the estates and give a discharge for the sale monies; otherwise the debts could not be paid.
How is it shown that the purchaser is relieved from the responsibility of ascertaining that all the testator's debts are paid before the completion of the purchase? and from the responsibility of seeing to the application of the purchase-money?	
9. Have any of the persons named in the abstract, to the knowledge of the vendor or her solicitor, been declared bankrupt or taken the benefit of any of the Insolvent Debtor's Acts? And if so, when?	But this is a case (an implied trust) which appears to be provided for by the 14th section of the Act 22nd and 23rd Vic., c. 35. The 23rd section of the same Act relieves the purchaser from the responsibility of seeing to the application of the purchase-money. The vendor is also executrix.
10. Has the tenant of the estate, Mr. , any lease or any written agreement regulating his tenancy, and has the vendor any counterpart or duplicate thereof, and is the same duly executed and stamped?	
The instrument (if there be any) should be abstracted	

Requisitions on behalf of Purchaser.	Replies of Vendor's Solicitor.
and produced, and delivered up to the purchaser on completion. What notice will be requisite to determine the tenancy?	
11. The succession duty, which became payable on the death of Richard Appleton, must be paid, and the receipt must be handed to the purchaser.	This will be done.
12. Are there any rights of way, or other easements affecting the property sold? If so, what are they? State the particulars.	
13. Is the vendor or her solicitor aware of any judgments, crown debts, annuities, lites pendentes, writs of execution, or any charge or incumbrance, or deeds or documents affecting the property or the vendor's title thereto, not disclosed by the abstract? If so, what are they?	The abstract has been prepared with reference to the provisions of the 24th section of the Act 22 and 23 Vic., cap. 35, and for the purpose of enabling the legal adviser of the purchaser to satisfy himself that a good title at law and in equity is deduced to the property sold; under these circumstances, and as a matter of practice the vendor's solicitor does not consider that he is bound to reply to this requisition, and that he cannot reasonably be required to do so.
They must be satisfied, or the property released therefrom by and at the expense of the vendor.	
14. The purchaser reserves the right of making any further objections or requisitions which may arise from the above, or the vendor's answer thereto.	
A—— B——, Purchaser's solicitor.	[Reply of purchaser's solicitor.—The question asked is one which is rarely omitted in requisitions on title. The purchaser is entitled to have a reply, either that the

Requisitions on behalf of Purchaser.	Replies of Vendor's Solicitor.
	solicitor of the vendor is or is not aware of any encumbrance affecting the title, other than those appearing on the abstract.]
	C—— D——, Vendor's solicitor.

No. 6.—ABSTRACT.

FREEHOLD TITLE.

BETTINSON'S TITLE.

Observations.

This title commences with a covenant to stand seized to uses by Robert Franklyn, made on the marriage of his son, Edward Franklyn, with Mary Denton.

A duly verified certificate of this marriage should be obtained, otherwise it will not appear that the contingent remainders limited by the settlement became vested remainders.

The recital of the death of Robert Franklyn in the recovery deed of 4th May, 1817, may be considered as sufficient evidence of that fact. It is stated that no entry of the proceedings under this recovery can be found, and that search has been made in all the superior courts; and that no exemplification of the recovery is with the deeds. The statute 14 Geo. 2, cap. 20, sec. 4, provides a remedy in cases where no record of a recovery can be found, and as at this period (1870), 50 years have elapsed since the death of Edward Franklyn, without issue, and as the title has been held adversely since 1819, it may be assumed that the claim of any of the persons (reversioners) claiming under the deed of 19th July, 1807, is barred.

Certificates of the burials or deaths of Mary Franklyn and Edward Franklyn, and a statutory declaration that they left no issue, must be produced, and evidence of their identity.

Joseph Bettinson by his will devised his estates to his wife for life, and after her death to Peter Hart and John Thorpe, in fee, upon trust that they or the survivor of them, or the heirs of the survivor, should sell; but there does not appear to be any power of sale in the "assigns" of the surviving trustee; if the power or trust for sale be not given to the "assigns" of the trustees or surviving trustee, Charles Kimber (as the devisee of trust estates in the will of Peter Hart) cannot execute the trust for sale, or make a title to the estate without the concurrence of the parties beneficially interested in the money to arise from the sale; and if the concurrence of the heir-at-law of Joseph Bettinson can be obtained, it will be desirable, or a bill must be filed and the sale made under a decree of the Court.

A certificate of the death of Isabella Bettinson should be furnished, and evidence of her identity.

Receipts for the succession duties which became payable on the deaths of Joseph Bettinson and Isabella Bettinson must be handed to the purchaser, or it must be shown that only legacy duty is payable on the estate. Searches for judgments, &c., must be made as against Joseph Bettinson.

See General Observations, No. 7, *et seq.* Some of these will be applicable to this title.

No. 7.—ABSTRACT.

FREEHOLD.

DENHAM'S TITLE.

Observations.

The title only commences in 1826 (44 years since). A title for 60 years must be deduced, and an abstract of the earlier deeds and documents must be furnished.

Inquiry must be made whether John Chapman, the vendor in the conveyance of 3rd November, 1826, was married at the date of that conveyance, and if so, whether his then wife or widow be now living; and whether John Chapman be dead, and when he died, and where he was buried. If he be living, or in case he has not been dead 20 years, his wife or widow (if living) is entitled to dower out of the estate (unless barred by settlement or other provision, which must be shown), and must release her dower.

It appears from the abstract and pedigree,

That Richard Sandall (the testator) died in November, 1853.

That Jane Sandall, his widow, is living. Jane Sandall is entitled to dower out of the estate (unless barred by settlement or some other provision, which must be shown), and she must concur in the conveyance to the purchaser to release her dower, or execute a release of dower previously.

That Jonathan Sandall (the tenant for life under the will of Richard Sandall) had issue two children only, who both died in his lifetime, under age and unmarried.

That Jonathan Sandall died in August, 1860, without leaving any issue him surviving.

That Maria Sandall married Benjamin Walton, and had issue only one child, a daughter, Frances Walton.

That Maria Walton died in 1856, in the lifetime of Jonathan Sandall, her brother,) leaving her daughter, Frances Walton, her surviving.

That Frances Walton attained 21 years of age, and died in July, 1858, without issue and unmarried.

That Benjamin Walton is living.

> Under the will of Richard Sandall, Maria Walton became entitled to one moiety of the estate as tenant in tail general in remainder, and she having died in the lifetime of her brother (the tenant for life), her husband, Benjamin Walton, did not on her death become seized of her moiety during his life as tenant by the curtesy of England; to complete the right of a husband to curtesy, the wife must have died seized in possession.

That Eliza Sandall (who under the will of the testator became entitled to the other moiety of the estate as tenant in tail general in remainder) married Charles

Darwin, and had issue one child, Samuel James Darwin, and died in February, 1862.

That Charles Darwin and Samuel James Darwin are both living.

Eliza Darwin survived her brother Jonathan Sandall, and her sister and niece, who died leaving no issue, and, under the limitation of cross remainders in the will, Eliza Darwin became entitled to the other moiety (making the entirety) of the estate as tenant in tail general in possession, and on her death her husband Charles Darwin became entitled to the entirety during his life as tenant by the curtesy.

Under the 22nd section of Act B, Charles Darwin, as tenant by the curtesy, became protector of the settlement created by the will of Richard Sandall, and as Charles Darwin did not (as protector) concur in or consent (conformably to the Act) to the disentailing deed of 9th November, 1863, the effect of that deed was only to bar the estate tail and to create a base fee in Samuel James Darwin, and the remainder in fee over was not barred. It is stated that Samuel James Darwin is a bachelor; if he dies without issue, and without having converted the base fee into a fee simple by a proper assurance, or when his issue fails, the base fee will determine and the estate will go over and belong to the person entitled to the remainder in fee under the will. 3 & 4 W. 4 cap. 74.

The conveyance of 29th May, 1864, only passed the base fee. The purchaser cannot accept a base fee.

As Charles Darwin and Samuel James Darwin are stated to be both living, the vendor (if the purchase proceeds) must complete his title to the fee simple before the conveyance to the intended purchaser. The vendor must obtain a proper assurance and conveyance from Charles Darwin (as tenant by the curtesy, and protector) and Samuel James Darwin to the vendor, so as to convert the base fee into a fee simple, which deed must be duly enrolled in Chancery.

An abstract or draft of the proposed deed must be furnished to the purchaser's solicitor.

Unless this conveyance and confirmation be obtained the purchaser must decline to complete.

The objections to the joining of Charles Darwin and Samuel James Darwin in the conveyance to the intended purchaser, are—

1st. The length of the conveyance will be increased.
2nd. The cost of enrolling the deed.
3rd. The costs of the solicitor of the Darwins in perusing the draft and obtaining their execution, &c.

These costs must be paid by the vendor.

If the purchase be proceeded with, the following evidence must be required and furnished, and searches and inquiries made:—

1. Receipts from the Inland Revenue Office for the succession duties which became payable on the respective deaths of Richard Sandall, Jonathan Sandall, and Eliza Darwin (the succession duty payable in respect of the death of Eliza Darwin will become payable on the death of Charles Darwin, and must be commuted for and paid by the vendor).

2. Duly authenticated certificates of the marriages of Jonathan Sandall, Maria Walton, and Eliza Darwin.

Of the births of Frederick Sandall, Caroline Sandall, Frances Walton, and Samuel James Darwin.

And of the deaths of Frederick Sandall, Caroline Sandall, Jonathan Sandall, Maria Walton, Frances Walton, and Eliza Darwin.

3. Statutory declarations to the following effect by persons intimately acquainted with the family and identifying the parties—

> That Jonathan Sandall had no more than the two children before named, that they both died without issue and unmarried, and that Jonathan Sandall was only married once.
>
> That Maria Walton was only married once, and that she had no other child than Frances Walton; that Frances Walton died without issue and unmarried.
>
> That Eliza Darwin was only married once, and had no other child than Samuel James Darwin.

4. Searches must be made at the Public Record Office, Rolls Buildings, Chancery Lane, for any disentailing deeds and assurances by Maria Walton, Frances Walton, Eliza Darwin, and Samuel James Darwin; and as to Samuel James Darwin, search should be made for the last preceding year, at the Inrolment Office, Chancery Lane.

5. Searches should be made at the Common Pleas Office, Serjeants' Inn, Chancery Lane, as against Richard

Sandall, Frances Walton, Charles Darwin, and Samuel James Darwin, for judgments, crown debts, and lis pendens for the last five years; for annuities, for writs, or other process of execution under the Judgment Act, 1864, and for writs or other process under the Crown Suits Act, 1865, from the 1st November, 1865. And searches as against the same parties should also be made in bankruptcy and insolvency. And inquiries should be made of the vendor's solicitor whether any of the parties have been bankrupt or insolvent.

6. All the instruments abstracted should be produced and examined with the abstract; and it should be ascertained that all the deeds are properly stamped.

7. Inquiry must be made of the vendors and of their solicitor whether any money has been borrowed on the security of the estate, under the Drainage or Land Improvement Acts, and charged upon estate.

8. Receipts for all the outgoings, including the parish and other rates and assessments, must be produced upon completion of the purchase.

9. Inquiry must be made of the tenants as to the nature of their holdings, and whether any of them hold the property under a lease or agreement for a lease. If there are any leases or agreements, an abstract of them must be furnished; and inquiry should be made whether there are any rights of way or other easements affecting the estate; and also whether the tenants, or any of them, have any claim for acts of husbandry.

10. Inquiry must be made of the vendor's solicitor whether he has knowledge or notice of any deed, charge, lien, writ of execution, judgment, lis pendens, or incumbrance of any kind, affecting the property or title, which is not noticed or stated in the abstract.

11. The mortgage to Arthur Lorton must be paid off out of the purchase-money, and the mortgagee must concur in the conveyance to the purchaser.

No. 8.

FREEHOLD.

ADAMS' TITLE.

Observations.

Abstract, page 1.—The probate, or an office copy of the will of Jacob Smith must be produced to ascertain that Julia Mason (the wife of Joseph Mason) took an estate in fee simple under it, and also some evidence must be furnished of the seizin of Jacob Smith.

This having been the estate claimed as belonging in fee to a *feme coverte*, the conveyance in 1818 to Samuel Adams was, by the fine levied by Mason and wife—at that period married women could only convey their estates by fine or recovery.

Samuel Adams having died in 1830, his heir-at-law must be sought under the old law of inheritance, and as real estates would not then lineally ascend, and collateral relations of the half blood were excluded, the heir of Samuel Adams, at his death, appears (from the Adams' pedigree) to have been his great uncle, Titus Adams. Titus Adams by his will devised his real estates to his daughter Rebecca Adams, who (if living) appears to be the person now entitled to the estate.

The following certificates and evidence must be furnished, viz., certificates of the

Marriages of Adam Adams with Eliza Best.
Joshua Adams with Jane Thorpe.
Noah Adams with Mary Barnes and
Sarah Barton.
Births of Joshua Adams, Titus Adams,
Noah Adams, George Adams,
Samuel Adams, Maria Adams.
Deaths of George Adams, unmarried.
Sarah Adams.
Samuel Adams, unmarried.
Maria Adams, unmarried.

A statutory declaration must be furnished in support of the pedigree generally, and that none of the parties named in the pedigree had any other children than those stated in the pedigree.

Receipts for succession duty which became payable on the deaths of Titus Adams and Sarah Adams, to be furnished.

Searches to be made as against Rebecca Adams.

See General Observations as to leases to tenants and charges under Drainage and Land Improvement Acts, and General Observations No. 7, et seq.

No. 9.—ABSTRACT.

COPYHOLD TITLE.

DENTON'S TITLE.

Purchaser's Requisitions and Observations.	*Vendor's Replies.*
1. It appears from the abstract of the will of Charles Denton that it was only attested by one witness.	At the date of the will of Charles Denton (1832), a will attested by one witness only was sufficient to pass copyhold estates.
2. Was Jeremiah Denton separately admitted tenant on the court roll?	The admission of Sarah Denton, the tenant for life, was the admission of the party entitled in remainder.
3. What stamp is on this surrender?	
4. Did Jeremiah Denton surrender the copyhold estate to the use of his will?	At this time (1856) a surrender to the use of a will was not necessary.
5. Has the satisfaction of the conditional surrender to Richard Marton been entered on the court rolls of the manor? If not, the satisfaction must now be entered on the court rolls, in	Satisfaction shall be entered on the court rolls.

Purchaser's Requisitions and Observations.	Vendor's Replies.
respect of this mortgage surrender.	
6. It appears that Robert Denton (one of the devisees named in the will of Jeremiah Denton) died in 1860, in the lifetime of his father, the testator of 1856; therefore it is presumed that the devise to Robert Denton lapsed, and that a moiety of the copyhold estate descended upon the customary heir of Jeremiah Denton, the testator. What is the custom of the manor as to descent?	It is true that Robert Denton died in the lifetime of his father, Jeremiah Denton, the testator of 1856; but Robert Denton left issue four children who are now living. By the 33rd section of the Wills Act (Act E) gifts to children who leave issue do not lapse.
7. Assuming that the devise to Robert Denton did not lapse, it is very questionable whether, under the words of the devise contained in the will of Robert Denton, the fee of a moiety of the copyhold estate passed to Joanna Denton, his widow, or only an estate for her life: who is the customary heir of Robert Denton?	It is submitted that, under the devise contained in the will of Robert Denton of the whole of the testator's estate, the fee of the copyhold moiety passed to Joanna Denton, his widow; there can be very little doubt on this point on a reference to the cases collected in Jarman on Wills.
8. The court rolls of the manor must be carefully searched, to ascertain that the abstract is correct and complete.	The purchaser's solicitor can make this search.
9. Has any charge been made on the estate under the Drainage and Land Improvement Acts? Search should be made for any such charges.	
10. Are the vendors, or is their solicitor, aware of any surrender, charge, lien,	

Purchaser's Requisitions and Observations.	Vendor's Replies.

judgment, writ of execution, lis pendens, annuity, or any other incumbrances affecting the property, which are not disclosed by the abstract?

Search should be made for judgments, &c., as against Jeremiah Denton and the vendors. (See page 120.)

11. Have any of the persons mentioned in the abstract been bankrupt, or taken the benefit of any of the Insolvent Debtors' Acts, or executed any deed of composition with their creditors? And if so, when: state the particulars.

12. Is the farm under lease, or is there any agreement with the tenant?

If so, the lease or agreement must be abstracted and produced.

Inquiry on these points must be made of the tenants.

What notice to quit must be given to determine the tenancy?

Are there any rights of road or way over the estate, or any other easement affecting the property? If so, state them.

13. The following certificates must be furnished to the purchaser, viz.:—

    1. A certificate of the death of Sarah Denton on 9th August, 1840.

Purchaser's Requisitions and Observations.	Vendor's Replies.

2. A certificate of the death of Robert Denton on 4th November, 1860.

3. A certificate of the marriage of Robert Denton with Joanna his wife.

4. Certificates of the births of their three children.

5. A certificate of the death of Jeremiah Denton on 2nd February, 1866.

6. A certificate of the death of Maria Denton, the annuitant.

7. And a statutory declaration by a person or persons acquainted with the family, verifying the certificates and identifying the parties, and stating that Robert Denton left four children living at the time of his death.

14. The probates of the wills of Charles Denton and Jeremiah Denton, and the letters of administration to the estate of Robert Denton (with the will annexed) to be produced.

15. It must be shown who is the personal representative of Maria Denton, and, as such, entitled to receive the proportionate part of the annuity of £200 up to her

Purchaser's Requisitions and Observations.	*Vendor's Replies.*

death, and the arrears (if any).

16. The receipts for the succession duties which became payable on the death of Jeremiah Denton, must be produced and handed to the purchaser, and also the receipt for the succession duty which became payable on the cesser of the annuity of £200 on the death of Maria Denton, and a receipt from her personal representative, showing the payment of a proportionate part of the annuity up to her death, must be handed to the purchaser.

17. As the amount of the purchase-money is considerable, it will be desirable that the purchaser should have the usual covenants for title from Thomas Denton and Joanna Denton (as to their moieties), and that they should covenant as against their own acts, deeds, and incumbrances, and also as against the acts, debts, and incumbrances of Charles Denton and Jeremiah Denton.

This purpose may be effected by a deed of covenants for title of even date with the surrender.

No. 10.

ABSTRACT TITLE OF DERMER TO REVERSIONARY
INTEREST IN CONSOLS.

Observations and Requisitions on part of Purchaser.

1. The purchaser's solicitor must be satisfied that the £4,850 Consols are now standing in the names of Ashworth and Clift (the trustees of the testator's will), and that there is no distringas upon the stock which can affect the reversion proposed for sale. To enable the purchaser's solicitor to satisfy himself on these points, the trustees must furnish him with a letter to the chief accountant of the Bank of England. (See form of this letter, post.)

2. The purchaser must be satisfied that all the funeral and testamentary expenses and debts of Martin Oliver, the testator, and all the legacies given by his will, have been paid or satisfied.

3. The receipt for the legacy duty on the Consols must be produced, and a copy of it must be furnished to the purchaser.

4. The vendor must obtain a written admission from Ashworth and Clift (the trustees), that they hold the £2,425 Consols (one moiety of the £4,850) upon the trusts by the will of Martin Oliver declared concerning the £5,000 Consols, thereby given upon trust for Sarah Sanby for life, and at her death for Charles Sanby and Fanny Louisa Dermer.

5. The age of said Mrs. Sarah Sanby must be proved by the production of a certificate of her baptism or birth, and a declaration as to her identity, and her present address must be furnished.

6. A certificate of the marriage of Edwin Dermer with Fanny Louisa Dermer must be furnished, and a statutory declaration by some disinterested person as to their identity; the certificate should be marked as an exhibit to the declaration.

7. The probate of the will of Martin Oliver, and the deed of 4th March, 1868, must be produced and in-

spected by the purchaser's solicitor; and an office copy of the acknowledgment of the deed by Mrs. Dermer must be furnished to the purchaser.

8. The deed of 4th March, 1868, or a part of it (if it has been executed in duplicate) should be handed over to the purchaser on completion. If it has been executed in duplicate, a memorandum of the assignment to the purchaser must be endorsed on the part retained by Mr. Dryden (the trustee of the deed). Was notice of the assignment of 4th March, 1868, duly given to the executors and trustees of Mr. Oliver's will?

9. The vendor (Mr. Dermer) must make a statutory declaration stating that he has never been bankrupt, or taken the benefit of any of the Insolvent Debtors' Acts, or assigned, or charged, or in any way dealt with his reversionary interest, or done any act which will prevent him from assigning his interest to the purchaser; a draft of this declaration should be submitted to the purchaser's solicitor before it is made.

10. Application must be made to the Reverend Mr. Ashworth and Mr. Clift (the trustees of the testator's will), and to Mr. Dryden, to inquire whether they have received notice of any charge by Mr. Edwin Dermer or his wife on the Consols, or any dealing with the Consols by either of them beyond the settlement abstracted. (See form of letter.)

11. The purchaser's solicitors should make the usual searches for proceedings in bankruptcy and insolvency, and for composition deeds with creditors as against Mr. Edwin Dermer, and also for any judge's charging order on the stock, and for lis pendens against the trustees of the will.

12. Mr. Dryden must concur with Mr. Dermer in the assignment to the purchaser.

13. If the purchase be completed a writ of distringas must forthwith be issued and placed upon the stock at the suit of the purchaser.

14. Formal notice in writing of the assignment must be forthwith given to the trustees of the will.

> Form of Letter to Chief Accountant of Bank of England, requesting information as to any distringas on Stock. (This letter must proceed from one of the Trustees in whose names the Stock is standing) :—

"To   , Esq.,
   "Bank of England.

"Sir,—I shall be obliged if you will give Mr. A—— B——, of   , such information as he may require, with respect to the sum of £4,850, £3 per cent. Consols, now standing in the names of myself and the Reverend Francis Ashworth, and as to any distringas or other charges thereon.

"I am, Sir, your obt. servt.

"ALFRED CLIFT."

Form of Letter of Inquiry to the Trustees of Fund and Executors of Will of the Testator. (N.B.—This Letter of Inquiry should be sent to all the trustees of a fund.) :—

"Gentlemen,

"Mr. Edwin Dermer, of No.   Road, has proposed to sell to my client, Mr.   , the reversionary interest of Mr. Dermer (expectant in possession on the death of Mrs. Sarah Sanby, of No.   Street), in £2,425 Consols, being a moiety of £4,850 Consols, which is stated to be now standing in your joint names as the trustees and executors of the will of Mr. Martin Oliver, late of   .

"Mr. Dermer states that his interest in the fund is derived under a settlement made by himself and his wife, Mrs. Fanny Louisa Dermer, dated 4th March, 1868.

"On the part of the proposed purchaser, I request the favour of your informing me, whether all the funeral and testamentary expenses and debts of Mr. Martin Oliver, the testator, and all the legacies bequeathed by his will, have been paid, and whether the above-mentioned sum of £4,850 Consols is now standing in your names as trustees of the will of Mr. Martin Oliver, upon the trusts by his will declared concerning a sum of £5,000 Consols, thereby directed to be held for the benefit of Mrs. Sarah Sanby during her life, and after her death for the absolute benefit of Charles Sanby and Mrs. Fanny Louisa Dermer, in equal moieties; and whether this sum of £4,850 Consols stands by itself, or forms part of any, and what larger sum of stock; and whether the legacy duty on this stock has been paid, and if so, out of what fund it was paid; and whether you have received notice, or are aware of any assignment or of any charge or incumbrance, or any bankruptcy or insolvency, affecting the share of Mrs. Fanny Louisa Dermer, or her husband Mr. Edwin Dermer, of and in such sum of stock, or of any circumstance which would prevent their dealing with their reversionary interest in the stock.

"It will oblige Mr. and Mrs. Dermer if you will sign the enclosed letter to the Chief Accountant of the Bank of England, describing the stock, and requesting him to afford me information whether there be any distringas or charge on the stock, or any judge's order affecting the stock.

"I shall be willing to pay your solicitor's charges for his trouble in replying to this letter on your behalf.

"I am, &c.,

"To { Rev. Francis Ashworth.
{ Alfred Clift, Esq."

In case the trustees do not make any reply to the application to them for information, a letter similar to the following can be written to them :—

"Gentlemen,

"On the   ulto., I forwarded a letter to you with reference to the reversionary interest of Mr. Edwin Dermer, of No.   Road, in a sum of £2,425 Consols (a moiety of a sum of £4,850 Consols now standing in your names as trustees of the will of the late Mr. Martin Oliver, of   ), and as to any notice you may have received of any dealings with or charges on such moiety of stock.

"I have not received any reply from you to my letter. I regret very much to occasion you trouble, but I shall be much obliged if you or your solicitor will favour me with a reply to my letter before the   instant ; and I beg to inform you that if I do not receive a reply on or before that day, I shall assume that you have no notice or knowledge of any charge or incumbrance upon or dealing with Mr. or Mrs. Dermer's moiety of the stock, and shall act accordingly.

"It would, however, be more satisfactory to me to have a written reply from you. I have no wish to give you personally the trouble of writing a reply; it will be equally satisfactory if you write through the medium of your solicitor, whose charges I shall be willing to pay.

"I am, &c.,

"To Rev. Francis Ashworth and
"Alfred Clift, Esq."

Statutory Declaration by Vendor.

I, Edwin Dermer, of No.   Road, in the county of   , do solemnly and sincerely declare:

That I have never been bankrupt, or taken the benefit of any of the Insolvent Debtors' Acts, and that I have not assigned or charged, or in any way dealt with the reversionary interest of my wife Fanny Louisa Dermer, or any interest in her right (except by an indenture of settlement, dated the 4th day of March, 1868, executed by myself and my said wife, and duly acknowledged by her), or otherwise in or relating to a moiety of £5,000 Consols, or other the fund for the time being representing the same, to which my said wife became entitled in reversion (expectant on the death of her mother, Sarah Sanby), under the trusts of the will of Martin Oliver, late of   , deceased; or done any act which will prevent me from absolutely assigning my interest in such moiety of Consols or other the fund for the time being representing the same, to Mr.   , the proposed purchaser.

And I make this solemn declaration, &c.

Notice to Trustees of Assignment.

"To the Reverend Francis Ashworth and Alfred Clift, Esq. (trustees of the will of Martin Oliver, late   , of   , deceased).

"I hereby give you notice, that by indenture dated the   day of   , 1872, made between Edwin

Dermer, of   Road, in the county of   ,
of one part, and   of   , of the other
part, it is witnessed, that for the consideration therein
expressed, the said Edwin Dermer assigned to the said
                    absolutely, all that the sum of £2,425
Consols, part of a sum of £4,850 £3 per cent. Consolidated Annuities, now standing in your joint names as trustees of the will of Martin Oliver, Esquire, in the books of the Governor and Company of the Bank of England, or other the stocks, funds, or securities, into or in which the said sum of £4,850 Consols, or the produce thereof, or any part thereof, may be converted or invested under the power for that purpose contained in the said will of the said Martin Oliver, and the dividends and income of such sum of £2,425, or other securities for the same, after the decease of Sarah Sanby (the sister of the said testator), and to which said moiety of stock, and the dividends and annual income thereof, the said Edwin Dermer is now entitled in reversion (subject only to the life interest of Mrs. Sarah Sanby, and expectant on her decease). To hold the same unto the said   , his executors, administrators, and assigns, absolutely.

"I shall be obliged by your acknowledging the receipt of this notice, and am,

"Your obedient servant,

"A—— B——,

"Solicitor for the said
"(purchaser.)

"(Date and residence.)"

No. 11.—ABSTRACT.

LEASEHOLD FOR YEARS.

MORGAN'S TITLE.

Requisitions on part of a Purchaser.

1. In what office have the houses been insured, in

whose names, and in what amount ? the policy must be produced, and the receipt for the last premium.

2. To whom is the ground rent of £30 reserved by the lease now payable ? State the name and address of the party.

The receipt for the last quarter's ground rent must be produced to the purchaser.

3. By the will of Robert Thornton, these leasehold houses were specifically bequeathed to the testator's daughter, Mary Robinson, for life, and after her death in trust for her children.

Is Mary Robinson living, or if dead, had she any children ?

For what reason were the leaseholds sold by Pember, the executor ? Inquiry should be made whether Pember (the executor) assented to the specific bequest of the leaseholds.

It appears that Pember never proved the will of Robert Thornton, and that the other executor renounced probate. Mrs. Catherine Thornton, the administratrix, with the will annexed, should now concur in the assignment to the purchaser. What amount of stamp duty was paid on the letters of administration ?

4. Have any of the parties named in the abstract, viz., Robert Thornton, Jonathan Latham, or Clement Morgan, to the knowledge of the vendor, or his solicitor, been bankrupt, or taken the benefit of any of the Insolvent Debtors' Acts ?

If so, when ? [Search should be made by the purchaser's solicitor.]

5. The receipt for the succession duty which became payable on the leaseholds on the death of Robert Thornton must be produced.

6. A printed copy of the rules of the Permanent Mutual Benefit Building Society, and a printed copy of the certificate of the barrister appointed to certify such rules, should be furnished, and it must be shown that the rules of the society were duly approved and certified by the barrister, and that the society was duly constituted.

7. A certified copy of the resolution, or written instructions of the board of directors of the building society, directing the sale of the property, should be furnished to the purchaser.

8. A certificate of the death of C. (one of the mort-

gagees and one of the trustees of the society) should be furnished; and also a certificate from the secretary of the society, and a copy of the resolution of the board, or some other official document, showing that Mr. D. has been duly appointed to be one of the trustees of the society, should be furnished.

9. By what statute, and section, is the mortgage relieved from stamp duty?

10. Have any leases been made to the tenant of either of the houses, or any agreements? If so, the leases or agreements must be abstracted and produced. [Inquiries on these points must be made of the several tenants.] What notice to quit must be given to the tenants?

11. Are there any mortgages, charges, leases, judgments, lis pendens, crown debts, writs of execution, or other incumbrances affecting the property, or any part of it, which are not disclosed by the abstract? [Searches for judgments, &c., should be made by the purchaser's solicitor.]

Replies by Vendor's Solicitor.

To Requisition 3.—It is a general rule of law and equity, that an executor has an absolute power of disposal over the whole personal estate of his testator, and that it cannot be followed by legatees, either general or specific, into the hands of the alienee. The principle is that the executor in many instances must sell in order to perform his duty in paying debts, &c., and no one would deal with an executor, if liable afterwards to be called to account. In this case the sale was made by the executor very soon after the death of the testator. See Williams on Executors, 5th Edition, 838, 839.

To Requisition 6.—One of the conditions of sale is, that the production of a printed copy of the Rules of the Benefit Building Society, and a printed copy of the certificate of the barrister appointed to certify such rules, shall be conclusive evidence that such society was legally constituted in all respects, and in cases where the vendor has not such copies, it shall be assumed that the societies were legally constituted in all respects—that all parties who acted as trustees of such societies shall be assumed to have been properly appointed, without any evidence; and all proceedings of such persons shall be deemed to have been regular. And all acts done or to be done by them shall be assumed to be authorised and valid.

To Requisition 9.—10 Geo. IV., c. 56, sec. 37.

No. 12.—ABSTRACT.

LIFE POLICY.

Observations.

In the case of this policy it appears that a claim is made for the payment of the sum assured not only by the executrix of the will of Mr. Shapland, the mortgagee of the policy, but also by Messrs. M—— & O——, the solicitors acting for Mrs. Wrayson, the administratrix of the estate of the assured.

On the part of the assurance company,

1. It must be ascertained by statutory declaration that the Rev. Tobias Wrayson, who in the policy is described as of Hastings, is the same person as the Tobias Wrayson who is described in the deed of 3rd November, 1866, as of   , and who died at   , on the 29th day of July, 1870.

2. It must be ascertained by search that neither the Reverend Tobias Wrayson or Mr. Arthur Shapland or his widow have ever been bankrupt, or taken the benefit of any of the Insolvent Debtors' Acts.

3. It appears that Mrs. Louisa Shapland is in possession of the policy, and therefore, under the mortgage of 3rd November, 1866, she can give the company a discharge for the claim.

4. With reference, however, to the letter of Messrs. M—— & O——, it will be proper to write to those gentlemen intimating that the claim will be paid to the executrix of the mortgagee on a certain day (say a week after the claim shall have become actually due and payable), unless they shall in the meantime show sufficient

cause to the contrary. If no answer is received to this communication, it will be requisite to preserve evidence of the delivery of such letter to Messrs. M—— & O——.

5. The mortgage of 3rd November, 1866, and the policy, with certificate of Mr. Wrayson's death, should be handed to the assurance company.

6. The probate of the will of Mr. Shapland should be inspected; and it must be ascertained that the probate stamp is of sufficient amount to cover the sum assured and the bonus now payable on the policy.

No. 13.

FREEHOLD TITLE.

Observations.

Prior to the reading of this abstract it will be instructive to the student to read carefully the canons of descent as stated by Sir William Blackstone, in his Commentaries, 2nd volume—which may be referred to as the old law of inheritance; and then to read Act D, which came into operation on 1st January, 1834, and which defines the new law of inheritance, and particularly section 6.

DAYRELL AND LYDFORD'S TITLE.

These are two pedigree titles; and the title to the estate depends upon the evidence which can be adduced in support and proof of the accuracy and completeness of the statements in the pedigrees; and various certificates and other evidence of marriages, births, and deaths, and other facts, will be requisite to be called for and furnished in support of the abstract and pedigrees.

It must be ascertained whether Thomas Mantell (the vendor in 1807) was married at the date of the conveyance by him, and whether his wife or widow be now living; and when Thomas Mantell died (if dead). If he has not been dead more than twenty years, his widow (if

152   ABSTRACT No. 13.

living) may be entitled to dower. It sometimes happens that even at this long distance of time (64 years) a widow of a former owner may be living who is entitled to dower.

The probates of the wills of Isaac Dayrell and Robert Lydford must be produced, and carefully compared with the abstract.

The following duly authenticated certificates must be furnished:

1. Of the marriages of
   Timothy Dayrell with Mary Johnson.
   Isaac Dayrell with Maria Carter.
   Sarah Dayrell with Reuben Lydford.
   Charles Lydford with Mary Dealtry.
   Thomas Lydford with Celia Rutter.
   Reuben Lydford (twice).

2. Of the births of
   Isaac Dayrell.   Sarah Dayrell.
   George Dayrell.   William Dayrell.
   Susan Dayrell.   Joseph Dayrell.
   Jane Dayrell.   Christopher Lydford.

3. Of the deaths of
   George Dayrell.   Reuben Lydford.
   Maria Dayrell.   Isaac Dayrell.
   Joseph Dayrell.   William Dayrell.
   Sarah Lydford (née Dayrell). Jane Dayrell.
   Christopher Lydford.   Thomas Lydford.

A statutory declaration or declarations by a person or persons intimately acquainted with the families generally in support of the pedigrees and of the facts therein stated, and particularly showing

That George Dayrell, William Dayrell, Joseph Dayrell, Jane Dayrell, and Robert Lydford (the testator),
all died unmarried.
    That Isaac Dayrell, Sarah Dayrell, and Thomas Lydford,
were respectively only married once, as appears by the pedigrees.
    That Reuben Lydford was only married twice, as appears in pedigree.

That Reuben Lydford had no other child than Christopher Lydford.

And that Timothy Dayrell, Isaac Dayrell, and Thomas-Lydford had no other children than those named in the pedigree.

As to the Dayrell Moiety.

Sarah Lydford (as a devisee in the will of her father, Isaac Dayrell) became entitled in fee in remainder to one half of this moiety by purchase, and she became entitled to the other half by descent as the heir-at-law of her sister, Jane Dayrell.

Sarah Lydford (the wife of Reuben Lydford) having died in the lifetime of her mother, Maria Dayrell (who was tenant for life of this moiety), and having only an estate in fee in remainder in this moiety, and never having been in possession, her husband, Reuben Lydford, did not on her death become entitled to this moiety as tenant by the curtesy; and on the death of Sarah Lydford the Dayrell moiety descended upon her son, Christopher Lydford.

As Sarah Lydford appears to have died under 21 years of age, she was not able to dispose of or charge this moiety, therefore it will not be necessary to search for a fine or recovery as levied or suffered by her.

Christopher Lydford died in 1833, before Act D came into operation; and upon his death, an infant, this moiety descended upon his aunt, Susan Dayrell, who was his heir-at-law according to the old law of inheritance (but subject to life estate of Maria Dayrell); therefore Susan Dayrell, who by the pedigree appears to be living, became (on the death of Maria Dayrell) entitled in fee simple in possession to this moiety.

As to the Lydford Moiety.

Reuben Lydford, who was seized in fee simple in possession of this moiety by purchase under the will of his uncle, Robert Lydford, died without any issue surviving him, and intestate; but leaving a widow. It appears from the pedigree that he was the only child of Thomas Lydford.

Reuben Lydford having died in 1865, his heir-at-law must be sought for under the new law of inheritance,

154 ABSTRACTS NOS. 13 AND 14.

3 & 4 W. 4,
cap. 106.
Act D, section 6. And this heir appears to be his grandfather, Charles Lydford, who (according to the pedigree) is now living. On the death of Reuben Lydford intestate, his widow, Rebecca Lydford (unless barred of dower by declaration or some other mode, which must be shown) became entitled to dower out of this moiety.

Therefore (as to the Dayrell moiety), Susan Dayrell will be the party to convey, and (as to the Lydford moiety) Charles Lydford will be the party to convey, and Rebecca Lydford to release her dower; and these three persons can make a good title to the entirety of the estate, subject to the former observation as to the widow (if any) of Thomas Mantell.

Succession duties.—Receipts for the succession duties which became payable on the deaths of Maria Dayrell (as to one moiety), and Reuben Lydford (as to the other moiety), must be produced and handed to the purchaser or mortgagee.

Searches for judgments, &c.

These searches must be made as against Reuben Lydford, Charles Lydford, and Rebecca Lydford, and Susan Dayrell. See General Observation, No. 7; and the other General Observations from No. 8, so far as they are applicable to this title.

No. 14.—ABSTRACT.

RYCROFT'S TITLE.

Observations and Requisitions on part of a Purchaser of Moiety of £15,000 New Three per Cents.

1. The interest of the vendors (Mr. and Mrs. Rycroft) being a reversionary interest in personalty vested in a *feme coverte*, the transaction can only be carried into effect by an assignment executed by Mr. and Mrs. Rycroft, and acknowledged by Mrs. Rycroft, under the provisions of the 21st Vic., c. 57.

2. It must be ascertained in whose names the £15,000 New Three per Cents. is now standing. It should be

transferred into the names of the executors and trustees of the will of Geoffrey Turville, or if Mrs. Miranda Turville and the other parties are all willing, or if the trustees think it expedient so to do, the stock may be transferred into Court under the provisions of the Trustee Relief Act.

3. It must be ascertained that there is no distringas or stop order, or judge's charging order on the stock. To satisfy the purchaser's solicitor on this point a letter must be furnished by the parties in whose names the stock is now standing to the Chief Accountant of Bank of England. (See form of this letter at page 144.)

4. The purchaser must be satisfied that all the funeral and testamentary expenses, and debts, of Sir Gilfred Turville and Geoffrey Turville, the testators, and all the legacies given by their wills, have been paid or satisfied.

5. The receipts for the legacy duties on the stock payable under the two wills must be produced, and copies of the receipts must be furnished to the purchaser.

6. The receipt for succession duty which became payable on the stock on the death of Lady Sheldon must be produced, and handed to the purchaser.

7. The vendors must obtain a written admission from the executors and trustees of the will of Geoffrey Turville that they hold the £15,000 stock upon the trusts by the will of Geoffrey Turville declared concerning his residuary personal estate.

8. The age of Mrs. Miranda Turville must be proved by the production of a certificate of her baptism or birth, and a declaration as to her identity; and her present address must be furnished.

9. A certificate of the death of Lady Sheldon, and certificates of the deaths of Arthur Lewis and Matthew Garner, and also a certificate of the marriage of Mr. and Mrs. Rycroft, should be furnished, and a statutory declaration as to their identity. The certificates should be marked as exhibits to the declaration.

10. A certificate of the birth of Lucy Turville should be furnished, and it must be seen that her age did not exceed 25 years at the date of the appointment of 7th December, 1850.

11. The probates of the wills of Sir Gilfred Turville and Geoffrey Turville, and the appointment of 7th December, 1850, and the deed poll endorsed must be

produced and inspected by the purchaser's solicitor, and it must be ascertained that the attestations of the deeds poll were signed, sealed, delivered, &c.; and attested copies of the two deeds poll, and a covenant for their production, should be obtained by the purchaser, and a memorandum of the assignment of a moiety of the stock to the purchaser should be endorsed on the two deeds poll.

12. The vendor, Mr. Rycroft, must make a statutory declaration stating that neither he nor his wife have ever been bankrupt, or taken the benefit of any of the Insolvent Debtors' Acts, or assigned or charged or in any way dealt with the reversionary interest of Mrs. Rycroft, or done any act which will prevent them from assigning their interest in the stock. A draft of this declaration should be submitted to the purchaser's solicitor before it is made.

13. Application must be made to the executors and trustees of the wills of Sir Gilfred Turville and Geoffrey Turville to inquire whether they have received notice of any charge by Mr. Geoffrey Turville, or by Mr. or Mrs. Rycroft, on the stock in question, or any dealing with the stock with any of them beyond the deeds abstracted. (See form of letter, page 144.)

14. The purchaser's solicitor should make the usual searches for proceedings in bankruptcy and insolvency, and for composition deeds with creditors as against Mr. Geoffrey Turville and Mr. and Mrs. Rycroft; and also for any judge's charging order on the stock, and for lis pendens as against the trustees of the wills.

15. If the purchase be completed, a writ of distringas must forthwith be issued, and placed upon the stock at the suit of the purchaser.

16. Formal notice of the assignment should be forthwith given to the executors and trustees of the will of Geoffrey Turville.

No. 15.

ABSTRACT OF THE TITLE OF MRS. CAROLINE HOLCOMBE
TO A POLICY OF ASSURANCE.

Policy of Life Assurance.—Equitable mortgagees.—
Administration suit.

Observations.

Policy No. 2,462.

Claim, Jasper Holcombe.

This Policy (No. 2,462), effected by Mr. Holcombe on his own life, was deposited by him in 1868 with Messrs. A—— B—— and Company, bankers, by way of security for the repayment of a loan, and an account current with them, and interest and bankers' charges.

The assured, by his will (dated in 1870), bequeathed all his personal estate to his wife, and appointed her sole executrix. She proved the will in March, 1872.

The probate of the will of Mr. Holcombe must be produced, and it must be ascertained that the amount of probate duty paid is of sufficient amount to cover the sum payable under the policy; subject to the payment of all principal and interest moneys which may be due to Messrs. A—— B—— and Company (who hold the policy), on their memorandum of deposit, the amount of the claim on this policy would become payable to the executrix of the will of the assured.

From the abstract it appears that a Bill has been filed in the Court of Chancery by a creditor of Mr. Jasper Holcombe for the administration of his estate under the direction of the Court.

The decree abstracted appears to be the ordinary decree, in common form, directing the usual accounts to be taken, and that the personal estate of the testator should be applied by the executrix in a due course of administration.

An office copy of the decree should be furnished and compared with the abstract.

If the decree be simply in the common form, the

amount of the claim may (with the written consent and authority of Messrs. A—— B—— and Company) be paid to Mrs. Holcombe, the executrix of the assured.

It must be ascertained by search that Mr. Jasper Holcombe (the assured) did not become a bankrupt, or take the benefit of any of the Insolvent Debtors' Acts.

The policy must be given up: if the full amount due to the bankers be satisfied, the memorandum of deposit should be handed to the insurance office, with the policy, or an endorsement made on the memorandum of deposit of the payment of the claim, and a separate undertaking to produce the security to the office.

No. 16.—ABSTRACT.,

LEASEHOLD FOR YEARS.

HARTON'S TITLE.

Requisitions on title on behalf of purchaser or intended mortgagee, and replies of vendor's solicitor.

Requisitions.

1. The ground comprised in the lease of 1st July, 1880, is described as a piece of ground situate in the parish of St.   , in the county of Middlesex. Evidence (by statutory declaration) must be produced, identifying the ground on which the ten houses sold have been built with the ground as described and comprised in the lease, and also as being the ground which has been laid out and is now known as part of Augusta Square, and the ten houses sold as being Nos. 1 to 10 in Augusta Square.

2. Office copies of the proceedings in the bankruptcy of Robert Chard and of the appointments of the official and creditors' assignees, must be produced and handed to the purchaser.

3. It has been stipulated that the title of Arthur Latimer (the lessor) shall not be required to be shown.

To whom is the ground rent of £50, reserved by the lease of 1830, now paid? State the name and address of the party.

The receipt for the last quarter's ground rent to be produced.

4. Under the covenant in the lease, no assignment was to be made without the written license of the lessor. The written consent of the lessor to the assignment of the lease to Thomas Parker must be produced and handed to the purchaser.

5. Has the assignment of the lease to Thomas Parker been registered in Middlesex? If not, it must now be registered.

6. Have any of the parties named in the abstract (besides Robert Chard), to the knowledge of the vendor or her solicitor, been bankrupt, or taken the benefit of any of the Insolvent Acts?

Did Robert Chard take the benefit of any of the Insolvent Debtors' Acts? and if so, when?

7. It must be shown that the will of Matthew Parker was signed by him and attested by two witnesses. The probates of the wills of Thomas Parker and Matthew Parker must be produced.

8. What amount of probate duty was paid on the two wills abstracted? it must be ascertained to be to the full amount of the property sold. If not, a further probate duty must be paid.

9. Have the wills of Thomas Parker and Matthew Parker been registered in Middlesex? If not, they should be registered, and the particulars of the registry should be furnished to the purchaser's solicitor.

> [Reply.—These wills have not been registered; it is not usual to register wills, unless they contain a devise of a freehold estate. In this title the lease was registered, and the assignment to Thomas Parker will be registered; and a further title cannot be made without giving notice of the wills, unless something should appear on search of the registry.]

10. Are the annuitants, Maria Watson and Clara Parker, named in the will of Thomas Parker, or either

of them, now living? If living, they must join in the assignment and release the property. If both, or either of them, be dead, certificates of their deaths and evidence of their identity should be furnished, and receipts or admissions must be produced of the payment of the annuities, and receipts from the representatives of each or either annuitant (if dead) for a proportionate part of the annuity, up to the date of their respective deaths, must be produced.

11. The succession accounts and receipts for duty, in respect of the devolution of the property from Thomas Parker to his son, Matthew Parker, and in respect of the devolution of the property from Matthew Parker to his sister, Martha Harton, must be produced; and also the succession accounts and receipts for duty, in respect of such of the annuities as have ceased, or the succession duties in respect of the annuities must be commuted for, if the annuitants be living.

12. In what insurance office are the houses insured, and for what amount, and in whose names? The policy or policies must be produced, and also the receipts for the last premiums.

13. Have any leases been made to, or agreements entered into with, the tenants of any of the houses? If so, the leases or agreements must be abstracted and produced.

Inquiries on these points must be made of the several tenants.

What notice to quit must be given to the tenants?

14. Are there any mortgages, charges, leases, assignments, judgments, lis pendens, crown debts, writs of execution, annuities, or other incumbrances affecting the property, or any part of it, which are not disclosed by the abstract?

A—— B—-—,
Purchaser's solicitor.

N.B.—The usual search should be made in the Middlesex Registry.

No. 17.—ABSTRACT.

FREEHOLD.

PARKES' TITLE.

This title commences with a lease in 1780 for 999 years—a long term.

In 1830 the termor assigned the term to a trustee to attend the inheritance, and then made a feoffment and levied a fine to acquire a tortious fee;· in the deed assigning the term, it is stated that the reversioner was not then known. It will be requisite to have a statutory declaration that no rent has been paid during a long term of years last past.

If the title be accepted, a title must be shown to the term, and the term must now be assigned to a trustee for the purchaser; as it is apprehended that the term did not cease under the provisions of the Act 8 and 9 Vic., cap. 112; that Act only applies to freehold, and certain customary estates, and not to leasehold estates. See 3rd section of the Act.

Under the will of Edward Parkes, his three sons took as tenants in common in fee.

As to Jeremiah's third.

By the settlement 28th June, 1840, made on the marriage of Jeremiah Parkes, his third was (subject to the life estates of Jeremiah Parkes and Charlotte Benson) limited to the use of the issue of the marriage. In a deed the word "issue" is not a word of limitation; and it is apprehended that the effect of the settlement was to give only life estates in this third to the three children of the marriage, and that (subject to the life estate of Mrs. Charlotte Parkes) the three children are now entitled to this third during their lives as tenants in common in remainder. Subject to their life estates, this third is vested in Mrs. Parkes in fee under Jeremiah's will.

As to Rowland's third.

Rowland Parkes by his will devises his one-third to his brother, Jeremiah, and his children; the effect of which, it is apprehended, was to give them the fee simple as tenants in common.

Jeremiah Parkes by his will devises his real estates to his wife Charlotte.

Therefore, as to Frederick's one-third, he will be the party to convey.

And as to the other two thirds, Mrs. Charlotte Parkes and her three children will be the parties to convey, according to their respective interests. The usual evidence must be furnished as to the marriage of the parties, births and number of children, and deaths of parties. (See No. 18.)

The usual searches for incumbrances must be made as against all the conveying parties. See General Observation, No. 7.

And see also General Observations, No. 8, and all the following observations so far as they are applicable to this estate and title.

No. 18.—ABSTRACT.

SPEARTON'S TITLE.

Observations.

The vendors in this case are stated to be the next of kin of Miss Margaretta Spearton, who is stated to have died in 1871, an infant and unmarried.

The property stated to be purchased is the reversionary interest of her next of kin (expectant in possession on the death of Mrs. Frances Welford, the widow of Basil Welford, whose age is stated to be 74), in 40 shares of £100 each in the L—— and W—— Bank, and £4,000 East India Railway debentures, constituting part of the residuary personal estate of Mr. Basil Welford.

Margaretta Spearton, the infant legatee named in the will of Robert Spearton, appears to have been at her death absolutely entitled to the funds in question, subject to the life interest of Mrs. Frances Welford.

From the pedigree of the Spearton family (if correct) it would appear that Martha Spearton, the aunt *exparte paterná*, and Louisa Waters, the aunt *exparte materná*, of Margaretta Spearton, are her next of kin, and absolutely entitled to her personal estate, and to take out administration to her effects.

1. Letters of administration of the personal estate of Margaretta Spearton must be obtained, and must be produced, and it must be ascertained that the proper amount of stamp duty is paid on them. The sale and assignment will be by the administrator.

2. The probates of the wills of Basil Welford and Robert Spearton must be produced, and carefully compared with the abstract, and it must be ascertained by inquiry of the executors whether all legacy and succession duties have been paid. The receipts must be produced.

3. The age of Mrs. Frances Welford must be proved by the production of a certificate of her baptism or birth, and a statutory declaration of her identity, and her present address and residence, must be furnished.

4. Certificates of the following facts must be furnished, of

Marriages of	Christopher Spearton,
Do.	Samuel Spearton,
Do.	Joshua Waters.
Births or baptisms of	Samuel Spearton,
Do.	Robert Spearton,
Do.	Martha Spearton,
Do.	Margaretta Spearton,
Do.	Thomas Spearton,
Do.	Richard Spearton,
Do.	Charles Welford.
Deaths of	Christopher Spearton and of his two wives, and evidence that he was only married twice, and that neither he or either of his wives had any other children than those named in the pedigree.
Do.	Robert Spearton, and evidence that he died a bachelor.
Do.	Charles Spearton,
Do.	Thomas Spearton,
Do.	Richard Spearton,
Do.	Charles Welford, and evidence that he died under 21.
Do.	Margaretta Spearton, and evidence that she died an infant and unmarried.

5. And a statutory declaration or declarations by some person or persons well acquainted with the several families, as to the above facts, and identifying all the parties. The certificates must be marked as exhibits to the declaration.

6. The vendors must obtain a written admission from Mr. Raymond Welford and Mr. Richard Clare that they hold the bank shares and railway debentures upon the trusts by the wills of said Basil Welford and Robert Spearton declared thereof.

7. The purchaser must be satisfied that all the debts of Basil Welford and Robert Spearton, and the legacies given by their wills, have been paid; and these facts must be ascertained by application to, and inquiry of, the several executors and trustees of the wills of Basil Welford and Robert Spearton.

8. The power to appoint new trustees in the will of Mr. Basil Welford, and the trust or power in the same will for the investment and variation of the securities for the trust funds, must be fully set out on the abstract, and the appointment of Richard Clare by the indenture of the 9th of June, 1870, must be fully abstracted, and it must be seen that the power was properly exercised, and that no variation of the trust securities has taken place with respect to the bank shares or the railway debentures contracted to be sold.

9. The vendors must make a statutory declaration stating that neither of them nor Mr. Robert Spearton have been bankrupt, or taken the benefit of any of the Insolvent Debtors' Acts, or assigned or charged, or in any way dealt with the reversionary interests now sold, or done any act which will prevent them from assigning their interests to the purchaser. A draft of this declaration should be submitted to the purchaser's solicitor before it is made.

10. Application must be made to Mr. Raymond Welford and Mr. Clare, and to the executors of the will of Robert Spearton, to inquire whether any of them have received notice of any charge upon, or dealing with, or encumbrances affecting, the bank shares or railway debentures by any of the parties interested. (See form of letter, page 144.)

11. The purchaser's solicitor should make the usual searches for proceedings in bankruptcy and insolvency, and for composition deeds with creditors, and for any

judge's charging order, as against Robert Spearton and the vendors, and for lis pendens against the executors and trustees of the wills of Basil Welford and Robert Spearton.

12. If the purchase be completed, formal written notice of the assignment must be forthwith given to the executors and trustees of both the wills.

No. 19.—ABSTRACT.

COPYHOLD.

HADLEY'S TITLE.

Observations and Requisitions.

1. What is the custom of the manor of D——, as to freebench? Is any widow of James Hadley now living? If so, she should release her right to freebench.

2. What is the custom of the manor of D——, as to entails? Does the custom allow customary estates to be entailed?

3. What was the custom as to descent in 1812?

4. The court rolls of the manor should be carefully searched to ascertain that the abstract is correct and complete.

5. The probate or an office copy of the will of Jonathan Parker should be furnished, and it should be ascertained that his daughter Mary Parker was executrix, and proved the will, and that the proper probate stamp is on it to cover the £500 mortgage debt and interest.

6. Under the will of Christopher Phillips, the legal estate was devised to Benjamin Travis. The three children of Christopher Phillips were joint tenants in tail, of the equitable estate, with cross remainders.

7. The following certificates of facts must be furnished to the purchaser, viz. :—

Births of the three children of Christopher Phillips, to show their ages;
Deaths of Ada Phillips,
Charles Phillips,
Martha Phillips;
And a statutory declaration by some person or persons well acquainted with the family, identifying the parties, and verifying the certificates, and showing and stating that Ada Phillips and Charles Phillips both died infants, without issue, and unmarried; the certificates should be made exhibits to the declaration.

8. It must be shown that the deed of disentail of 23rd November, 1858, was duly entered on the court roll of the manor within six calendar months after the date and execution of the deed, otherwise the entail and the remainder over were not duly barred.

9. Receipts for the succession duties which became payable on the deaths of Martha Phillips, Ada Phillips, and Charles Phillips, must be produced and handed to the purchaser on completion.

And it should be ascertained that the probate and legacy duties which under the will of James Hadley became payable in respect of the purchase-money for the estate are paid.

10. The conveyance to the purchaser will be by a bargain and sale, from the executors and trustees of the will of James Hadley; the purchaser will be entitled to admission on this bargain and sale. The copyhold estate is not devised to the executors, and they have a common law power to sell, therefore the executors cannot be admitted; but it should be ascertained that the lord of the manor has not seized the estate, *quousque*, for want of a tenant.

11. What documents of title will be handed to the purchaser on completion?

12. What are the outgoings payable out of the estate? it should be seen that all the outgoings, rates, and taxes are duly paid.

See General Observations and Requisitions applicable to this title.

No. 20.—ABSTRACT.

LEASEHOLDS FOR YEARS.

DORNTON'S TITLE TO LEASEHOLD ESTATE.

Requisitions of Purchaser's Solicitor.	*Replies of Vendor's Solicitor.*
1. In what office have the houses been insured, in whose names, and to what amount? The policy must be produced, and the receipt for the last premium.	The property is insured in £2,000 in the Fire Office. The policy and receipt will be produced.
2. To whom is the ground rent of £40, reserved by the lease of 29th September, 1840, now payable? State the name and address of the party. The receipt for the last quarter's rent must be produced to the purchaser's solicitor.	Mr. A—— B——, of No. street. The receipt will be produced.
3. Was Heinrich von Kohn, the lessee in the lease of 29th September, 1840, an alien? If so, had he been naturalized?	Henrich von Kohn was an alien, but obtained a certificate of naturalization from the Secretary of State under the provisions of 7 & 8 Vic. c. 66. This will be produced. See also Act 33 Vic. c. 14.
4. It appears that Radford and Hensley, the mortgagees, were Trustees of the Permanent Benefit Building Society; under what authority were they authorized to receive the mortgage debt of £400 and interest, and give a receipt for it? A copy of the authority from the directors or trus-	Under the rules of the building society.

Requisitions of Purchaser's Solicitor.	Replies of Vendor's Solicitor.
tees of the society must be furnished.	
Under what authority were the mortgagees authorized to indorse a receipt on the mortgage, and what is the effect and purport of that receipt?	A certificate from the secretary of the building society will be obtained as to the authority of the trustees.
Will the mortgagees concur in the assignment to the purchaser?	This will not be necessary; the receipt endorsed on the mortgage revested the property in the mortgagor. (See 5th section of 6 & 7 Wm. 4, c. 32.)
A printed copy of the rules of the Benefit Building Society, and a printed copy of the certificate of the barrister appointed to certify such rules, must be furnished to the purchaser.	(Copy certificate.) "I hereby certify that the foregoing rules are in conformity to law, and within the provisions of the statute 6 & 7 Wm. 4, cap. 32. "John Tidd Pratt."
There is no stamp on the mortgage. How is it exempted from stamp duty?	Under sec. 4 of 6 & 7 Wm. 4, c. 32.
5. Have any of the persons named in the abstract been bankrupt, or taken the benefit of any of the Insolvent Debtors' Acts? or executed any assignment to trustees for the benefit of creditors? If so, when? [N.B.—Searches in these respects should be made by the purchaser's solicitor.]	
6. The lease to H. von Kohn of 29th September, 1840, appears to have been an under-lease, and that the ground comprised in that	

Requisitions of Purchaser's Solicitor.

lease was part of certain ground comprised in the original lease of 25th March, 1840, and that Thompson, the lessor in the lease abstracted, was only a lessee. The property now purchased (with the other property comprised in the original lease) appears to be subject to a large annual rent and to the performance of covenants reserved and contained by and in the original lease. Unless, therefore, a satisfactory indemnity can be furnished by the vendor, the purchaser cannot be compelled or advised to complete his contract; it will be for the purchaser to determine whether or not he is disposed to take the title —the contract provides that the title of the lessor shall not be required to be shown, or objected to.

7. Are there any mortgages, leases, charges, deeds, judgments, lites pendentes, annuities, writs of execution, crown debts, or other incumbrances affecting the property sold which are not disclosed by the abstract? If so, state the particulars.

[N.B.—Searches should be made for these incumbrances in the proper offices, and in the Middlesex Registry.]

Replies of Vendor's Solicitor.

170 ABSTRACT No. 20.

Requisitions of Purchaser's Solicitor.	*Replies of Vendor's Solicitor.*
8. Maria Dornton, the annuitant mentioned in the will of Richard Thomas Dornton, must concur in the assignment to the purchaser, and release the property from her annuity, and the succession duty payable on her death must be commuted for.	
9. The receipt for the succession duty which became payable on the death of Richard Thomas Dornton in respect of the property now sold, must be produced and handed to the purchaser.	
10. Has the will of Richard Thomas Dornton been registered in Middlesex?	It is not usual or necessary to register wills with respect to leasehold estates for years. (See Sugden, Vend. and Pur., vol. ii., page 676, 11th edition.)

Extracts from Clauses in Acts relating to Mortgages to Trustees of Benefit Building Societies.

Under the Benefit Building Societies' Act, 6 & 7 Wm. 4, c. 32, sec. 4 (which incorporates the provisions of the Friendly Societies' Act, 10 Geo. 4, c. 56, sec. 37), mortgages by members of a Benefit Building Society to the Society, were exempted from stamp duty.

Since the 31st July, 1868, and under the 31 & 32 Vic., c. 124, sec. 11, the amount of the money to be secured by an unstamped mortgage to a Benefit Building Society is limited to £500.

All receipts endorsed on the mortgage deed are exempt from duty.

By 5th section of 6 & 7 Wm. 4, c. 32, it is enacted, " That it shall be lawful for the trustees named in any mortgage made on behalf of such societies, or the survivors or survivor of them, or for the trustees for the time being, to endorse upon any mortgage or furthe charge given by any member of such society to the trustees thereof for monies advanced by such society to any member thereof, a receipt for all monies intended to be secured by such mortgage or further charge, which shall be sufficient to vacate the same, and vest the estate of and in the property comprised in such security in the person or persons for the time being entitled to the equity of redemption, without it being necessary for the trustees of any such society to give any reconveyance of the property so mortgaged; which receipt shall be specified in a schedule to be annexed to the rules of such society, duly certified and deposited as aforesaid."

General Observations and Requisitions which may be applicable to various Titles.

The circumstances and facts relating to each title must, of course, be duly ascertained and considered.

No. 1.—Legal fee outstanding in a trustee.

Under the limitation in the   of   , 18 (or under the will of   ), the legal estate in fee simple would (unless it has been got in) appear to be outstanding in A—— B——, or his devisee or heir-at-law.

This legal estate must now be got in.

Is A—— B—— alive ?

If dead, when did he die ? and where was he buried ?

A certificate of his death or burial, duly authenticated as to identity, must be furnished.

If dead, did he make a will, or die intestate ?

If he made a will, the probate, or an office copy, must be produced, to ascertain whether it contains any devise which passed the legal fee simple vested in him as a trustee.

If A—— B—— died intestate, this should be shown by the production of letters of administration of his personal estate, or other evidence of his intestacy ; and if he died either wholly intestate, or intestate as to real estate vested in him as a trustee, it must be shown by proper evidence who is his heir or heirs-at-law. The nature of this evidence will depend upon the peculiar circumstances under which the party claims to be heir-at-law.

A—— B—— (if living), or his devisee of trust estates (if he made a will, devising trust estates), or his heir-at-law (if he died intestate as to freehold trust estates), must now concur in the conveyance of the legal estate in fee simple to the purchaser or mortgagee. If the trustee or heir be a *feme covert*, her husband must concur in the conveyance, and the wife must acknowledge the deed; and it must be ascertained that the parties are 21 years of age.

No. 2.—Dower of women married before 1834.

Inquiry should be made whether the vendor, or testator, or intestate (as the case may be), in 18 , was married at the date of the deed or death of the owner of the estate, and also whether his wife (if married before 1834) is now living, in which case it would appear that she is entitled to dower out of the estate, unless barred of dower by some mode which must be shown, or unless the vendor, testator, or intestate has been dead more than twenty years since (1871), in which case (if dower had not been claimed) it may be assumed that the widow is barred of dower by the 2nd and 3rd sections of Act A.

If the wife or widow is stated to be dead, a certificate of her burial or death, and evidence of her identity, should be required.

N.B.—This observation is applicable to women who were married before 1834, but it only applies to cases where the husband during the coverture had a legal estate either in fee simple or in fee tail in possession.

No. 3.—Dower of women who have been married since 1833.

A woman married since 1833 is entitled to dower out of all freehold estates of which her husband dies seized in fee simple or fee tail (whether legal or equitable) in possession, unless barred of dower by declaration or by deed or will of the husband. See Act C.

On the death of a person seized of a freehold estate in fee simple or fee tail in possession, it will be requisite to inquire if he left a widow; if so, she should release her right to dower (unless barred as above).

As to copyhold estates, the right of a wife or widow to freebench is not affected by the Dower Act (C). And on any dealing with a copyhold estate of inheritance in possession it will be requisite to inquire as to the custom of the manor with respect to freebench; and whether any widow of any former copyhold tenant be living. See Doe v. Gwinnel, 1 D. & G., 180; 1 Adol. & Ellis, N. S. 682; 6 Jur. 235; 10 Bing. 29.

N.B.—Inquiry with respect to widows entitled to dower or freebench is frequently overlooked and omitted to be made.

No. 4.—Succession duty.

Receipts must be produced showing the payment of the succession duties which became payable on the deaths of [state the names of the deceased parties]. The receipts must be handed to the purchaser on completion of purchase.

This only applies to persons becoming entitled on the death of any person dying since the 19th May, 1853.

In ordinary cases, this requisition may be shortly stated thus : " Succession duty receipts under the intestacy of A——, and also under the will of B——, must be produced, and handed to the purchaser on completion."

No. 5.—Search for deeds of disentail by tenants in tail.

A strict search must (shortly before the completion of the purchase or mortgage) be made in the Chancery Inrolment Office, Chancery Lane (for recent disentailing deeds), and at the Public Record Office, Rolls Buildings, to ascertain whether any deeds of disentail or assurances, or fines or recoveries, have been executed, levied, or suffered by any of the parties entitled to estates tail under any of the deeds or wills abstracted, viz. : [here state the names of the tenant in tail, or several tenants in tail, as the case may be].

N.B.—At the end of each year or half-year, an index of deeds of disentail and other deeds enrolled, and the records, are transferred from the Chancery Inrolment Office to the Public Record Office.

No. 6.—Enrolment of conveyances by tenants in tail.

The conveyance of mortgage must (as to the shares of) [state the names of the tenant or tenants in tail] be enrolled in Chancery within six calendar months after the execution of the deed professing to bar the entail, conformably to the provisions of section 41 of the Fines and Recoveries Act, 3 and 4

William 4 c. 74 (Act B); and the vendor or mortgagor must pay the cost of enrolment, unless the parties entitled to estates in tail bar the entail (by a short deed or deeds duly enrolled) before the conveyance or mortgage to the purchaser or mortgagee, which would save the expense of enrolling the conveyance or mortgage; in which case an abstract of the deed or deeds of disentail must be furnished, and the deeds produced; and it must be ascertained that they are duly executed and stamped, and also duly enrolled within six months after execution.

No. 7.—Searches for judgments, &c.
The usual search must be made (in the Common Pleas Office, Serjeants' Inn, Chancery Lane, London) for judgments, lites pendentes, crown debts, registered decrees, orders of Courts of Equity and Bankruptcy, writs of execution, and annuities, and at the Bankruptcy Court in Basinghall Street, in bankruptcy and insolvency (and at the Insolvent Registry in Portugal Street for insolvencies prior to 1860), and also for deeds of composition with creditors at the office of the Registrar of Deeds of Arrangements in Bankruptcy, No. 2, Quality Court, Chancery Lane, as against [here state the names of the parties as against whom these searches should be made.]

These searches should be deferred until a few days before the completion of the purchase or mortgage.

N.B.—With respects to judgments, registered decrees, orders of Courts of Equity and Bankruptcy, and other orders having the effect of judgments, which have been obtained or made since the passing of the Act 23 and 24 Vic. c. 38 (23rd July, 1860), and which did not exist at the time of the passing of that Act, it may be considered that they are not available, or of any force, unless duly registered in the Common Pleas Office, and unless a writ of execution or other process has been issued and put in force within three months after registry.

See sections 1 and 5 of the Act 23 and 24 Vic., c. 38 (Act K).

See also 2nd section of 27 and 28 Vic., cap. 112, as to judgments, &c., entered up since 29th July, 1864.

By that Act no judgment, &c., entered up after that date is to affect any land of whatever tenure, until such land shall have been actually delivered in execution by virtue of a writ of elegit, or other lawful authority, in pursuance of the judgment; the writs are to be registered.

It must, however, be kept in mind that the abovementioned Acts do not affect judgments entered up prior to the passing of those Acts.

Judge's charging orders on stocks, shares, &c.

If any person against whom any judgment shall have entered up in any of Her Majesty's superior courts at Westminster, is interested in any government stock, funds, or annuities, or any stock or shares of or in any public company in England, whether incorporated or not, standing in his own name, in his own right, or in the name of any person in trust for him, or in the name of the Accountant-General of the Court of Chancery, or is interested in the interest, dividends, or annual produce thereof, a judge of one of the superior courts may, on the application of any judgment creditor, order that such stock, funds, annuities or shares, or the interest, dividends or annual produce thereof, or such of them, or such part thereof respectively, as he thinks fit, shall stand charged with the payment of the amount for which judgment has been so recovered, and interest thereon; and such order entitles the judgment creditor to all such remedies as he would have been entitled to if the charge had been made in his favour by the judgment debtor; but no proceedings can be taken to have the benefit of the charge, until after the expiration of six calendar months from the date of the order. (Vide 1 and 2 Vic., c. 110, s. 14; 3 and 4 Vic., c. 82, s. 1.)

The order *nisi*, when passed and entered, should be served on the debtor, his attorney, or agent (sec. 15), and be lodged with the Accountant-General, if it affects a fund in court; and be served upon the Chief Accountant of the Bank of England, if it affects any government stock not in court; and, where it affects stocks or shares of any public company, it should be served on the authorised agent thereof (1 and 2 Vic. c. 110, sec. 15).

Every judgment debt carries interest at the rate of £4 per cent. per annum from the time of entering up the judgment (sec. 17).

No. 8.—Bankruptcy or insolvency.

Have any of the parties named in the abstract, to the knowledge of the vendor or his solicitor, been bankrupt, or taken the benefit of any of the Insolvent Debtors' Acts? or executed any deed of composition with creditors? And if so, when? State the particulars.

No. 9.—Searches for charges under Drainage or Land Improvement Acts (principally applicable to farms and large estates).

Searches must also be made at the office of the Inclosure Commissioners (at present at No. 3, St. James's Square, London) for any charges on the estate under the Drainage and Land Improvement Acts; and inquiry must be made of the vendors and their respective solicitors as to their knowledge of any such incumbrances.

No. 10.—As to leases to, and agreements with, tenants.

Are there any leases to, or agreements with, any of the tenants of any part of the estate? If so, they should be abstracted and produced; and it should be ascertained that they (or the counterparts) are duly stamped. What notices will be requisite to determine the tenancies? Are there any, and what, claims for compensation to be paid to the tenants, or any of them, for acts of husbandry done by them? Inquiry should be made of the several tenants whether they hold under any lease or agreement, and as to the terms of their holdings, and whether they hold as tenants from year to year, or how otherwise.

N.B.—Notice to a purchaser of a lease or tenancy, is notice of the contents of such lease, or the terms of such tenancy.

No. 11.—Easements.

Are there any rights of way, or other easements over, out of, or affecting any part of the estate sold? If so, what are they? State the particulars.

No. 12.—Stamps.

It should be ascertained that all the deeds and documents of title abstracted are properly stamped.

No. 13.—Inquiry should be made of the vendor's solicitor whether he or the vendor is aware of any judgment, crown debt, annuity, lis pendens, lease, mortgage, writ of execution, bankruptcy or insolvency, or any charge or incumbrance, or deed or document, affecting the property or the vendor's title, and not disclosed by the abstract.

In ordinary cases the requisition may be shortly stated thus: "Has the vendor been bankrupt or insolvent, or executed any conveyance or assignment for the benefit of creditors? and is the vendor's solicitor aware of any incumbrance affecting the property sold to Mr. A——?

No. 14.—What deeds and documents of title will be handed to the purchaser on completion?

No. 15.—Are there any outgoings payable out of the estate? If so, state the particulars.

No. 16.—It must be shown that all the rates and taxes and outgoings payable out of or in respect of the property sold, have been duly discharged.

No. 17.—The purchaser reserves the right of making any further objections or requisitions which may arise from the above requisitions or the vendor's answers thereto.

www.ingramcontent.com/pod-product-compliance
Lightning Source LLC
Chambersburg PA
CBHW032147160426
43197CB00008B/805